Bad English

"Language is funny, and so is Ammon Shea. His excellent new book tours our irrational prejudices about language, showing that an appreciation for the quirks and ironies of language history can put our understanding on a firmer basis and restore our sense of humor." —David Skinner, author of *The Story of Ain't*

"On the playground of language, there is no more mischievous laddie than Ammon Shea. I plan to use his new book to split the lip of the next insufferable language prig who saunters into my office to accuse me of bad English." —Roy Peter Clark, author of *The Glamour of Grammar* and *How to Write Short*

"In *Bad English*, Ammon Shea wastes no time challenging widely held beliefs about just what English is bad. His subtitle, 'A History of Linguistic Aggravation,' gets in an opening jab at sticklers like me, who know that 'irritate' means 'annoy' while 'aggravate' means 'make worse.' Shea, having read the OED to write *Reading the OED*, is well qualified to tell us we probably don't know as much as we think we do." —*The Washington Post*

"Have a look at Mr. Shea's taxonomy of peeving, and then examine your own conscience." —*The Baltimore Sun*

"Shea has done a terrific job of cutting through superstition and hearsay with fact after fact. If you're annoyed by so-called language lovers whose love consists of crabbing about everything, you will love this book." —Mark Peters, Vocabulary.com

"A very welcome addition to the canon of usage commentary . . . an outright success." —Stan Carey

bad
english

A History of Linguistic Aggravation

AMMON SHEA

A Perigee Book

A PERIGEE BOOK
Published by the Penguin Group
Penguin Group (USA) LLC
375 Hudson Street, New York, New York 10014

USA • Canada • UK • Ireland • Australia • New Zealand • India • South Africa • China

penguin.com

A Penguin Random House Company

Perigee trade paperback ISBN: 978-0-399-16558-0

The Library of Congress has cataloged the Perigee hardcover edition as follows:

Shea, Ammon.
Bad English : a history of linguistic aggravation / Ammon Shea.
pages cm
ISBN 978-0-399-16557-3 (hardback)
1. English language—Errors of usage—Dictionaries.   2. English language—Usage—
Dictionaries.   3. English language—Slang—Dictionaries.   4. English language—
Obscene words—Dictionaries.   5. Invective—Dictionaries.   6. Vocabulary.   I. Title.
PE1460.S5173   2014
428.2—dc23   2014005397

PUBLISHING HISTORY
Perigee hardcover edition / June 2014
Perigee trade paperback edition / June 2015

PRINTED IN THE UNITED STATES OF AMERICA

10   9   8   7   6   5   4   3   2   1

Text design by Laura K. Corless

For Alix and Ogden,
my pluperfect and future perfect both.

contents

introduction

Linguistic pet peeves require two things in order to survive and flourish: constant maintenance and the blood of a freshly wounded language. If the people who are peeved about a perceived language misuse do not remain vigilant, the issue is likely to slip from the awareness of the general public. And if the misuse is not repeated often enough, the peeve becomes irrelevant.

Anything that is worth fighting over is also worth celebrating. The aim of this book is to examine a number of the issues commonly thought of as mistakes in English usage and to see how these mistaken forms have been used over the past five hundred years in ways both eloquent and awkward. It is presented as a history of the things that we think are correct, the reasons why we think them so, and a celebration of the marvelously flexible language that has allowed room for such myriad forms.

According to those who sit up at night worrying about the state of our language, English has been headed to hell in a hand basket for a very long time. From the stubborn continuity of English, however, it seems clear that either (a) we are in an exceedingly slow hand basket or (b) the language will not break, no matter how willfully we mistreat it.

For hundreds of years we have been hearing a familiar litany of complaints: The language is being weakened by foreign imports, the failure to distinguish between similar words will lead to some devastating lack of specificity, young people are debasing the language with slang, Americans are ruining the King's English, improper grammar will lead to an inability to communicate beyond the most basic level of grunts. Yet in spite of all the indignities that we have heaped upon the English language, it continues to thrive and grow in rather magnificent fashion.

A good number of the complaints that one hears about language use—such as avoiding overly long words—have been constant for hundreds of years. Many others—such as the distinction between *shall* and *will*—have largely fallen by the wayside and now appear to us as historical curiosities, rules about which we scratch our heads and wonder why they once had people so bothered. Some complaints are modern creations, such as the hand-wringing over how the Internet and the use of text messaging are robbing our youth of the ability to write or think in phrases that exceed 140 typographic characters. Throughout all of this there are but two things that have remained constant: The English language continues to change and a large number of people wish that it would not.

For five hundred years speakers of English have been arguing over, worrying about, and scolding each other about how the language should be used. These speakers are largely divided into two camps: those who suspect that they themselves misuse the language and feel insecure about it and those who think they do not misuse the language and feel rather irritated by those who do (although there is admittedly some overlap between these two groups). In the view of the latter group, a perfect world would have a uniform standard taught to everyone, and there would be some authoritative guide that could enforce linguistic perfection, a sort of almanac for the language that could instantly settle any dispute about the use of a word or turn of a phrase. But then English would not be English: Our language is a glorious hodgepodge that is the result of invasion, exploration, linguistic inventiveness, and yes, simple error. And the book you hold in your hands is not an attempt to turn our language into an almanac of lists.

This book is not concerned with telling you that some form of language you have long used is wrong and should be avoided. It will not provide you with a set of rules to follow, in order that you might avoid the murmured corrections that we have all heard when violating some oft-invoked rule, such as ending a sentence with a preposition. What it will do is examine the roots and histories of these cherished linguistic peeves.

We are all constantly judging the language skills of the people around us. In part this is because we wear our level of erudition on our sleeves, where words are concerned. If you sit down next to someone at a dinner party you are able to make some judgment on their language use within minutes, simply based on the words they use and the way they put their sentences together. That same person might well have a terrible grasp of science, history, or geography, but it would take a considerable length of questioning for you to figure that out. With their language you can come to a judgment quite quickly. We all carry around with us these judgments and biases, but rarely do we stop to look at where they come from and ask why there are certain things that bother us.

I became interested in the subject of linguistic pet peeves because of my ability to inflame them in others. I discovered, after

having written several books on obscure words, that in some ways
I was possessed of a spectacularly incompetent form of Standard
English. I routinely failed to observe many of the basic rules of
subject–verb agreement; I used the passive voice when I could have
used the active; employed words such as *decimate, enormity,* and
literally in unapproved fashions; began my sentences with *but* and
ended them with prepositions; and committed other errors innumerable.

Following a series of appearances on radio shows during which
I spoke on the subject of dictionaries, I began to receive a large
number of letters from concerned citizens who felt that I was
contributing to the decline of the English language. These letters
ranged in tone from the mildly disapproving to the apoplectic,
and I regret to say that none of them had the desired effect of
improving the way in which I use English.

I am of a somewhat contrarian nature and do not respond
well to rules that appear capricious, illogical, or which, when questioned, come with the explanation of "because you should not
do that." None of the admonitions I received caused me to rethink
the way that I used my language. However, in researching the
origins of these examples of linguistic aggravation, I found that
learning the *why* of the problem did cause me to pay attention to
it in a way that I never had before.

I cannot say that I now write or speak in flawless Standard
English; such a feat would be impossible. There has never been
anything close to agreement about what exactly constitutes correct
English usage. Furthermore, I have no desire to adhere to many
of these rules, and I am entirely comfortable in using my language
the way that I want to use it. However, I can say that I now notice
when I am breaking many of these rules and take a delight in
feeling informed of the roots of my transgression.

If you are interested in asking questions about language and want to know why you have been told to not speak or write in a certain way, I hope that this book will give you answers and allow you to make a decision about whether you want to continue to annoy language purists in the future. And if you are one of these purists who is upset that I began this sentence with the word *and*, perhaps learning the history of this proscription will lessen your irritation with it.

I think it delightful that language can engender such passion. At the same time, I find the tendency to belittle people for verbal slights to be quite distasteful. I frequently hear people pointedly aver that they "care about language," which to me is simply a polite way of saying "I like to correct the language use of other people." We all care about language, some of us more than others, but the degree to which one is willing to humiliate or upbraid others should not stand as an indication of how much one cares.

A NOTE ON TERMINOLOGY

I have attempted to avoid, wherever possible, jargon and technical terms. In some instances it is unavoidable. One area that warrants explanation is the distinction between *grammar* and *usage*. Some time ago I observed a scrawl of graffiti in a bathroom stall, a Magic Markered conversation between two patrons. The first person had written "I'm literally dead," to which the second person responded with the imperative phrase "Learn grammar!" This respondent did not observe the distinction between the words *grammar* and *usage* that I do. In this book, *grammar* refers to the manner in which the language functions, the ways that the blocks of speech and writing are put together. *Usage* refers to using specific words in a manner that will be thought of as either acceptable or unacceptable. The question of whether or not to split an infinitive is a consideration of *grammar*; the question of whether one should use *literally* in a nonliteral sense is one of *usage*.

A NOTE ON PRONOUNS

I am well aware that the masculine form is preferred by many people, especially those who like to read books on language, when referring to an unnamed party in the third person. I am also aware that this has not always been the case in English. The third-person neuter singular (*they* or *their* when used to refer to a single person of either sex) was in common and accepted use until the beginning of the nineteenth century,[1] and is showing signs of making a resurgence. It is, in my view, a fine option for those who do not wish to always refer to unnamed people as *he*. I have opted to use the gender-neutral *they* in the singular, except where to do so would provide a lack of clarity or euphony.

A NOTE ON NOTES

This book makes use of both endnotes and footnotes. The former are intended for those brave souls who would like to find out additional information on the sources referenced. The latter function as parenthetical asides and are used in places where it would be awkward to place the information in the main body of the text. You should feel free to ignore either or both.

one

Arguing Semantics

The nine words discussed in this chapter are all examples of words that have not only become unmoored from some earlier meaning but have done so in a manner that has annoyed many people.

Almost all words change their meanings. This is one of the aspects of language that is firmly established. It ought to be evident to all of us that words will take on new meanings, as we generally find it confusing to read writing that is more than a few hundred years old: Many of the words carry a different significance than we give to them today.

Even the most dogmatic language purist accepts this concept. They may wistfully look back on some long-ago time as being the Edenic period of our language, but they will not attempt to start a conversation in Chaucerian verse as they know no one would understand them. Yet accepting that semantic drift occurs and liking it are not the same thing.

One of the things that is most curious about people who hold themselves up as language purists is that they seem to spend considerably more time complaining about language than they do celebrating it, much as if an art lover focused all their efforts on diatribes about the painters who were ruining the medium rather than the ones who were advancing it. This tendency is particularly in evidence when we look at words that are evolving.

You will rarely, if ever, hear someone extolling the beauty of a word that has recently taken on some delicate new shade of meaning; it is far more likely that you will hear them complain that the word is losing its specificity or losing its meaning altogether. However, it is frequently the case that the meaning being defended is not actually the original meaning of the word in question, merely the one that is preferred by the person doing the defending. The problem with attacking a word because of its semantic drift is that you run the risk of being hoisted on your own petard.

HOPEFULLY

> When someone says or writes, "Hopefully, the plan will be in operation by the end of the year," we know immediately that we are dealing with a dimwit at best.
> —Kingsley Amis, *The King's English*, 1997

> Started the day learning Mrs. Dwyer did not leave Iran—some snafu with paper work. Hopefully tomorrow.
> —Ronald Reagan, diary entry from February 8, 1981

In April 2012, the Associated Press announced, "We now support the modern usage of hopefully,"[1] which, in certain circles, was tantamount to saying "We now support beating baby seals to death with a copy of *Webster's Third New International Dictionary*." The fact that they made this announcement by tweeting it (as opposed to having the ghost of William Buckley read the proclamation from a vellum scroll in stentorian tones) served only to increase the ire of those who have long defended us from this onslaught against permissive semantic drift in our adverbs. The *Washington Post* fulminated, "The barbarians have done it, finally infiltrated a remaining bastion of order in a linguistic wasteland."[2]

What is this "modern usage" of *hopefully* that the AP referred to? In a nutshell, it is the word when used to indicate "it is to be hoped" or "I hope that," as opposed to the older sense, which is "in a hopeful manner." The ire expressed by the *Washington Post* is not an uncommon reaction to the expanded meaning of *hopefully*; few words in the twentieth century have had the power to so irritate people.

The 1975 *Harper's Dictionary of Contemporary Usage* gave a number of distinguished writers, academics, and public figures a list of words and phrases and asked them to comment on whether they found them acceptable or not. *Hopefully*, when used in the phrase "Hopefully, the war will soon be ended" elicited exactly the kind of sober and nonjudgmental responses that one expects from people opining on language use.

Phyllis McGinley, the Pulitzer Prize–winning poet, replied, "'Hopefully' so used is an abomination and its adherents should be lynched." T. Harry Williams, the famed biographer, wrote that it was "the most horrible usage of our time." Hal Borland, an author and journalist for the *New York Times*, said, "I have fought this for some years, will fight it until I die. It is barbaric, illiterate, offensive, damnable, and inexcusable."[3]

E. B White was far wittier than most of the members of the Harper's usage panel who condemned *hopefully* but had much the same reaction: "The first time we heard the word 'hopefully' used to mean something it doesn't mean was from the lips of a pretty woman whom we were wining and dining in a restaurant."[4]

This suppurating lesion on the face of the English language, the use of *hopefully* to designate "it is hoped that something will occur," has long been thought to be fairly recent. The *Oxford English Dictionary* (*OED*) currently has the earliest such use as 1932, when it appeared in the *New York Times Book Review*. Other dictionaries tend to not provide the date at which a secondary meaning of a word began, but we can guess that this sense was not in widespread use, if only because no one was complaining about it.

The "it is to be hoped" sense of *hopefully* makes no appearances in any of the guides for language use in the eighteenth or nineteenth centuries, or even until the middle of the twentieth. But when the language pundits do finally sit up and take note of it, they make up for not having seen it previously by attacking it with great vigor and gnashing of teeth.

There was a widespread opinion among these pundits that the "it is to be hoped" use of *hopefully* was recent.

As is so often the case, the practice that was being prescribed against happened to be considerably older than supposed. This use of *hopefully* may have not arisen until the middle of the twentieth century, but it certainly was in use before then and not, as many would have it, in an entirely faddish sense.

An article from the *Cleveland Plain Dealer*, from 1890, contains a quote from the president of the National Board of Fire Underwriters: "Losses are, however, on the increase, hopefully not as a permanent feature of the business."[5] We also can find it earlier in the nineteenth century, appearing in the *Dublin University Magazine* in 1838: "The day is hopefully not far distant when the rough irregularities of national peculiarities (so far as these peculiarities are offensive) will have rubbed one another away."[6]

But it was not entirely a creation of the nineteenth or even the eighteenth century. *Hopefully* reared its ugly head in the middle of the seventeenth century, in a translation of Montaigne's essays, printed in London in 1648: "This Discourse hath fully approved itself unto the Judgement of all those that have seen it hitherto, and hopefully it would have wrought some effect upon those that mannage the Affairs of this State, if the Danger of this last Commotion, had not employed all their strength and Attention, to save us from sudden Shipwreck."[7] In light of this example, it seems clear that the position of usage writers such as Roy Copperud ("until about 1960, the word was used only in the sense 'in hopeful way or feeling hope'")[8] is fairly unsupportable.

Why does *hopefully*, used in this nonstandard fashion, rub so many the wrong way? There have been a range of arguments made against it. One common argument used is the case against semantic drift, alleging more or less that the meaning "in a hopeful manner" got there first and so should be allowed to keep its position as the rightful meaning. But an appeal to change people's language habits based on first dibs is a difficult row to hoe. Other critics claim that this use of *hopefully* is incorrect because it is an adverb and adverbs should modify a verb, rather than a whole sentence. This argument has a certain kind of logic on its side, provided that the person doing the arguing is prepared to ignore that there are a large number of sentence-modifying adverbs that have been used in English for many hundreds of years.

The word *surely* often functions in much the same way that the disputed form of *hopefully* does. If one writes "Surely you are joking" the intended meaning is not "you are telling a joke in a manner that is sure." This use of *surely*, used to qualify a statement rather than a verb, has been in use since the late fourteenth century. *Truly*, in the sense of emphasizing a statement ("Truly, I had no idea she was your mother"), has a similar lineage, appearing in English with regularity since the late thirteenth century.

Sentence adverbs are quite useful and manage to convey different information than if the adverb were unnecessarily shackled to the verb. They have the ability to indicate some judgment on the part of the speaker, as can be seen in the two sentences "Regrettably, I said that" and "I said that regrettably." The first sentence means "I said something that I wish I hadn't," while the second means "I said something in a regrettable manner."

Yet another argument against this use of *hopefully* is that it makes no sense since the thing apparently being modified cannot feel hope, as when I write the words "This book will not, hopefully, be rent asunder by you when you read this chapter." "Aha!" cries the guardian of English, "the book cannot feel hope! Thus do I prove my case!" Somehow, in spite of this lexical incongruity, we manage to understand what people mean when they use the word in this manner.

One of the odder charges against the legitimacy of this usage was that it was nothing more than a bastard translation, inflicted upon the English language by a "hack translator." Wilson Follett, the author of *Modern American Usage*, was apparently under this belief and charged that the word had been translated from the German *hoffentlich*.[9] There have been other claims that *hopefully* is derived from a Yiddish or Dutch word or from another German term, *hoffnungsvoll*. These translation theories are inane enough that they make the final argument, which is "it makes you sound silly," seem quite reasonable.

Strunk and White's *Elements of Style* said of *hopefully* that while it "may be pleasurable and even useful to many . . . it offends the ear of many others who do not like to see words dulled and eroded."

If you care deeply about the opinion of people who would think less of you for using *hopefully* as a sentence adverb, then by all means, you should restrict yourself to "it is to be hoped" or a similar construction. Or you could avail yourself of one of the alternatives that have been suggested over the past few decades.

John Bremner, writing in *Words on Words*, recommended the use of *hopeably*, declaring that it had "begun to appear in respectable books, journals, magazines and newspapers and in conversation. . . . So, hopeably, the silly, offensive, ambiguous, sort, nonsensical, solecistic use of *hopefully* will diminish."[10] Bremner was either delusional, as there is no evidence of the word being used before him, or overly optimistic, as almost all of the subsequent written evidence of *hopeably* comes from writers who were making fun of him for suggesting it.

Others have recommended using *hopingly*, an obscure word that already exists in English. It is found mostly in older dictionaries, which tend to define it as "hopefully" (the older, and favored sense). However, the problem with using *hopingly* is that no one will know what you are talking about.

LITERALLY

People who use "literally" to mean "very" NEEDS TO DIE
—Title of discussion thread on actuarialoutpost.com, 2013

And when the middle of the afternoon came, from being a poor poverty-stricken boy in the morning, Tom was literally rolling in wealth.
—Mark Twain, *The Adventures of Tom Sawyer*, 1876

Among people who might be described as having at least a passing regard for the English language, there are few instances of usage that evoke a desire to mutilate more than the perceived misuse of *literally*. Whether the listeners/readers literally desire to mutilate those who misuse this word or whether they are literally hopping mad, I cannot say, but it docs seem as though this particular instance of semantic broadening leaves many people feeling particularly peevish. More so than almost any other word, *literally* has become the shibboleth that people who "care about language" wave about to show just how much they care. Such emotion in linguistic guardianship deserves closer regard.

The issue here is that some people (we might call them the Figurativists) use the word *literally* as an intensifier or in a figurative sense ("I literally vomited up my soul when you said that"), while others think that they should not do this ("No, you did not—souls cannot be vomited"). In fact, the second group of people (we may call them the Literalists) feel quite strongly about the matter: Many of them believe that such misuse of this word brands one as an imbecile and so lacking in couth as to be below pity. The Literalists are of the opinion that *literally* should never be used in place of *figuratively*. It should apparently never be used at all, unless, of course, one means to say that something happened in an extremely *literal* fashion.

One difficulty in assigning such strict meaning to *literally* is that it is unclear which meaning of the word should be applied. There have been a number of them over the past seven hundred years, including "without metaphor," "word for word," and "relating to letters or literature." However, the sense that is being defended here by the Literalists (used to denote "without metaphor") does appear to be the earliest use of this adverb. *Literally* has been used to mean "in a very exact, and not at all figurative, manner . . .

goddammit!" since the early fifteenth century, and perhaps we should give the word a gold watch for standing up against the onslaught of the godless Figurativist hordes for so long.

But this word is rather obviously the adverbial form of the earlier word *literal*, the earliest use of which was to indicate "relating to letters, or the alphabet," and this word is recorded in English prose several decades before *literally*. So we must accept that *literal* does not always mean the *literal* that we think it does or that we might want it to.

Another problem is that speakers of English, including some of our most celebrated authors, have been seduced into joining the ranks of the Figurativists (perhaps thanks to loose morals and a healthy supply of good whiskey).

When Vladimir Nabokov wrote, "And with his eyes he literally scoured the corners of the cell" in *Invitation to a Beheading*,[11] he obviously did not mean that the protagonist had removed his eyes from his head and used them to feverishly scrub the walls. Similarly, in the scene from *Tom Sawyer* in which Tom has bamboozled several neighborhood boys into performing the task of whitewashing the fence that his aunt Polly had set him to, and received in return many fine treasures,* we are given no indication that he was actually performing the action of rolling when Twain writes "Tom was literally rolling in wealth." And when we encounter the word in Theodore Roosevelt's description of the history of the Rough Riders ("we were literally deluged with applications"),[12] should we

----

* Including "twelve marbles, part of a jews-harp, a piece of blue bottle-glass to look through, a spool cannon, a key that wouldn't unlock anything, a fragment of chalk, a glass stopper of a decanter, a tin soldier, a couple of tadpoles, six fire-crackers, a kitten with only one eye, a brass door-knob, a dog-collar—but no dog—the handle of a knife, four pieces of orange-peel, and a dilapidated old window sash."

believe that there were actual streams of paper applications pouring over him? Of course not, and we have no difficulty understanding what he meant by it.

Literally has not yet fully assumed the status of being an auto-antonym (a word that means both one thing and its opposite, such as *splice*, which can mean both "to cut apart" and "to piece together"), although it is on its way. Does this mean that *figuratively* and *literally* are now interchangeable? No, it does not. No one is yet using *figuratively* to mean *literally*; the confusion, such as it is, is all in one direction.

If you count yourself among the Literalists, the bad news is that this particular usage is unlikely to go away any time soon. It has been used this way for about 250 years, and appears to be increasing in frequency. But English is a flexible language, and it generally is clear what people mean when they use *literally*, based on the context in which it is used. So the good news is that you will be able to understand what is being said, while at the same time basking in the warm glow of believing that the person with whom you are speaking has just literally (or figuratively, if you prefer) put their foot in their mouth.

DISINTERESTED AND UNINTERESTED

This is one of the worst of all American solecisms and it makes me boil.

—Anthony Burgess, in *Harper's Dictionary of Contemporary Usage*, 1975

He was rarely unkind to Saxon; but, on the other hand, he was rarely kind. His attitude toward her was growing negative. He was disinterested.

—Jack London, *The Valley of the Moon*, 1917

The two most common prefixes that we find attached to *interested* are responsible for provoking enough spleen to launch a thousand usage guides. Although rare, occasional uses of such forms as *deinterested* and *noninterested* can be found, particularly in writing from the nineteenth century. It is today widely considered (at least by the sort of people who stop to consider such things) that *disinterested* should mean "lacking bias" when considering a thing, whereas *uninterested* should mean "lacking interest" or "unconcerned with." Therefore, a judge would be described as *disinterested* (one hopes), and a student would be described as *uninterested* (one presumes).

The failure to properly affix these prefixes has led to countless examples of the sentence "*Disinterested* does not mean *uninterested*" appearing in such books as try to teach people how to write. While this statement is certainly true, without giving further explanation it is a little like saying "*Cat* does not mean *dog*." *Disinterested* and *uninterested* are different words, but it is not a simple matter of attaching a definition to each one and hoping that it sticks.

One may wish that *disinterested* retain the sense of "impartial" and that *uninterested* should forever mean "unconcerned with," but these are not the meanings that they have always had. In fact, in demanding strict adherence to these uses, one of the most beloved notions of some language purists (the proscription against semantic drift) is rather rudely trampled upon. For the original meaning of both of these words was the one that today is frowned upon.

According to current evidence provided by the *OED*, the earliest use of *disinterested* is found in 1631, when John Donne used it to mean "lacking interest." *Disinterested* did not pick up its modern hoped-for sense of unbiased for another several decades. The *OED* does specify that the use of *disinterested* to mean "without interest" is "often regarded as a loose use," which is notable, as it is the earliest use of the word. Someone must have come along at some point and decided that the word was created in error.

Uninterested likewise dates to the earlier portion of the seventeenth century and appears to have been first used by Walter Montagu in 1629 in *The Shepheard's Paradise*[13] to mean, unsurprisingly (dis-suprisingly?), unbiased, or "lacking bias."* *Uninterested* does not take on the modern meaning of "lacking interest, indifferent" until the latter half of the eighteenth century.

So it seems clear that each of these words began its life with the meaning that is widely considered today to be incorrect, and then the two met at some sort of unholy semantic swap meet and secretly agreed to change meanings, just to see if anyone would notice. No one appears to have paid much mind to the fact that each of these words were occasionally wearing the others' clothes, and for a while they were regarded, at least by some, as synonymous. A French–English dictionary from 1684 by Guy Miège, provides both words as definitions for the French *disinteressé*.[14]

Both *disinterested* and *uninterested* had variants that preceded them. The words *disinteressed* and *uninteressed* are found earlier in the seventeenth century, and each one of the *-ss-* words carried

----

* *Uninterested* is used three times in this work, in such contexts as "I have found here so uninterested a Counsellor, as he asks nothing but words to gratifie him; and he hath answered me so fitly, as if he had studied my cause before."

the same meaning as the first use of the -st- ones (what we now think of as the bad meanings).

Even though these two words are still frequently used interchangeably, most people do in fact observe a distinction. If you manage to fix these meanings in your head, there is no reason to not adhere to them, if only as a manner of simple politeness. If there is anything more arbitrary than insisting that *disinterested* and *uninterested* must always have entirely separate meanings it is insisting on using the original form of each word, just to show that you know what they meant in the seventeenth century.

DECIMATE

> Considering the obvious meaning of the word it is extraordinary how loosely it is often used. Even in the newspapers, and certainly in common talk, it is not infrequently employed to express great slaughter of a body of men, with a complete indifference to the proportion killed.
> —Basil Hargrave, *Origins and Meanings of Popular Phrases and Names*, 1911

> In doing so Morley decimated the notion that impurities in hydrogen gas were the reason the integral hypothesis could not be dismissed from the analytic chemistry lexicon.
> —Ralph R. Hamerla, *An American Scientist on the Research Frontier*, 2006

Here we have a classic example of a word that language enthusiasts love to wax furious about. The complaint typically centers on the fact that *decimate* is used improperly to refer to "destroying something or a large portion of something," when the "true" meaning of the word is "to put to death, or punish, one of every ten persons."

However, language has an irrepressible desire to change, and there are almost no words in English that have been around for more than a few hundred years without taking on new meanings, changing their old ones, or coming to simultaneously mean one thing and the opposite (a type of word known as an auto-antonym).

But the claim that *decimate* should mean nothing but "to put to death one of every ten" has deeper problems than that. For it is not at all clear that this militant meaning is indeed the earliest meaning of the word. There is another sense of *decimate*, meaning "to tithe," that is exactly as old—both senses date from the very beginning of the seventeenth century.*

The noun form of this word appears to be slightly older in English than the verb, with *decimation* (meaning a "tithe or taking of tithes") beginning to make appearances in English writing in the early sixteenth century, some seventy years before *decimate*.†

If we look to the dictionaries of this time period, the evidence suggests that this tithing sense of *decimate* was just as common, if not more so, as the sense of killing or punishing one of every ten. The first English dictionary to record the word was Thomas Blount's magnificently titled *Glossographia*, published in 1656, and it defines *decimate* as "to take the tenth, to gather the Tyth,"[15] with no mention made of killing or punishing anyone, soldiers or

----

* The earliest citation of *decimate* in a punishing sense dates from 1600, in a work by Ralph Carr, titled *The Mahumetane or Turkish historie*. *Decimate* meaning "to tithe" seems to make its first appearance in 1606, in a work by Henoch Clapham.

† The word appears in a book by William Barlow, printed in 1528: "To forge excommunicacions For tythes and decimacions Is their continuall exercyse."

otherwise. *Decimate* is next defined twenty years later in Elisha Coles's *An English Dictionary*, which records it as meaning both "to tythe or take the tenth" and "also punishing every tenth man."[16] These are the only two dictionaries of the seventeenth century to define *decimate* (which is not terribly surprising as there were very few such reference works at the time).

So given that these two meanings of *decimate* appeared almost simultaneously, why are we so invested in assigning the older Latin meaning to the word? It is because of the belief that the word entered English from the Latin word *decimatio*, which was a Roman form of military discipline, in which one of every ten men were punished (usually in response to a crime such as desertion). This is what is known as the Etymological Fallacy, a tendency to believe that a word's current meaning should be dictated by its roots. Insisting that this influence the current English meaning would make about as much sense as insisting that a *symposium* involve alcohol (it comes from a Latin word meaning "drinking partner") or that all *sinister* people are left-handed (since *sinister* meant "left" or "left hand" to the Romans).

The first concerned citizen to call foul on the extended use of *decimate* appears to have been Richard Grant White, in his 1870 book *Words and Their Uses*. White's clarion call to preserve the Romanesque meaning of the word did not meet with an immediate sigh of relief from language purists. Albert Ayres, a contemporary of White's who was just as big of a scold, turned up his nose at the notion that *decimate* should be used in any military sense, writing "This word, meaning as it properly does to tithe, to take the tenth part, is hardly permissible in the sense in which it is used in such sentences as, 'The regiment held its position, though terribly decimated by the enemy's artillery.'[17] But sometime after Grant's call to restore the Latin meaning of the word, a number of twentieth-century usage guides began to echo him. Judging by the fact that the broadened sense of the word has now been continually condemned for over a hundred years, it would appear that the people the language guides are directed at have not been paying attention.

It is not so surprising that *decimate* has proven itself to be resistant to being so pigeonholed in meaning. For not only is there the natural inclination of people wanting to use the word the way they see fit, there is also the problem that the prescribed meaning is a very narrow one. How often does one really have the need to say, in a single word or so, that something has had exactly one-tenth taken from it? Empirical evidence is lacking, but we must assume that this occurs substantially less than the need to say that something has had a largish amount taken, killed, stricken, and so on.

But there is another problem with restricting *decimate* to such a narrow meaning, which is that we have taken other exceedingly similar words and bent them to our desires. The word *ovation* entered the English language in much the same way as *decimate*, as its initial meaning was a historical Roman one, meaning something quite different than what it typically does today. The *OED* describes this sense of the word this way: "An ovation was given to a military commander who had either not defeated enough enemies to qualify for a triumph, or who had not achieved a complete victory, and included the award of a myrtle rather than a laurel crown, and a less spectacular procession."

At the beginning of the nineteenth century *ovation* began to be used in the context of "a great round of applause" and was frequently coupled with the word we most often see it alongside today, *standing*. It is unlikely that even the most exacting grammarian today would oppose the use of "standing ovation" in a nonmilitary context or when used to refer to a rapturous reception to a performance.*

ENORMITY

> Hurray for telling the muddlers how monstrous it is to use enormity where enormousness is meant.
> —Joshua Cohen, *The Globe and Mail* (Canada), March 25, 1978

> The enormity of You, a colossus!
> —Joyce Carol Oates, *Son of the Morning*, 1978

Several years ago, Barack Obama created a stir in the community of individuals who generally refer to themselves as people who "care about language." Not by issuing any socialist proposals, cutting funding for education, or misspelling a word—the issue was far more insidious: He repeatedly used the word *enormity* in a manner that many people thought improper.

In July 2008, while touring the Peterson Air Force Base in Colorado, Obama, at that time a candidate for president, spoke of "the *enormity* of the American accomplishment." And in January 2009, he gave a speech in which he spoke of "the *enormity* of the task that lies ahead."

"Obama Speech Sparks Misuse of Enormous Proportions"[18] read a headline in the *Chicago Tribune* on January 23, 2009, following one of these uses. Numerous letters were written about this

----

* Although this sense was excoriated by writers such as Ambrose Bierce, who in *Write It Right* stressed that the *ovation* should not be used for anything other than minor triumphs.

and his other uses of *enormity*; none of them was approving. Following Obama's acceptance speech, a man wrote sneeringly to the *Indianapolis Star*: "The word 'enormity' doesn't mean what President-elect Obama supposes, but it is very much appropriate to the policies he stands for."[19] Obama's use of this word even made it into some books: Simon Heffer, in *Strictly English*, observed rather primly that "One should not speak of the enormity of the task, but of its enormousness: even if one is President of the United States."[20]

The gist of the complaints about this word can be found in Heffer's remonstration: Many people feel that *enormity* should be used to refer only to a great evil and not to a great size. This is not a debatable point for such stalwarts; for them there is no possibility of semantic drift allowed, and one uses the word either correctly or not.[*]

But was Obama wrong? The assertions of his political detractors notwithstanding, this charge is a bit overstated. Answering the question requires that we look into the history of *enormity* as well as several related words, including *enormous* and *enormousness*. *Enormity* came into English as a loaner, as so many other bad habits supposedly did, from the French. The French word is *énormité*, which has had, like the English word, more than one meaning. The initial sense in French was for an "enormous crime" and began to be so used in the thirteenth century. The following century saw the word take on the additional meanings of

----

[*] I say this from personal experience, as I once intentionally used the word *enormity* to mean "something very large" in a book, just to see if people would complain. I have received more than fifty letters about this in the past few years, almost all of which were condemnatory. The few that were not vitriolic asked me if I had used it as a joke.

"something that exceeds boundaries" and "something of enormous size."

While *énormité* may have had a similarly ambiguous set of meanings in French, our Gallic cousins have apparently not been too bothered by this. All three meanings are currently in use in French, and prescriptive guides to that language, such as *Le Bon Usage*, contain no admonishments about the use of the word.

The earliest use of *enormity* now listed in the *OED* to designate "a great evil" is from 1477, in Caxton's printing of *The History of Jason*. The sense that irritates so many people is listed in that dictionary as 3a ("Excess in magnitude; hugeness, vastness"), and the earliest citation for this use is from 1792, which would seem to indicate that it is a relative newcomer to the scene. The *OED* itself engages in what might be wishful thinking, noting that this sense is obsolete, and that while "recent examples might perhaps be found . . . the use is now regarded as incorrect."

But it has been a number of decades since this entry in the *OED* has been edited, and previous editors on the dictionary have overlooked some earlier uses of *enormity* to refer to something large. Thomas Elyot uses it this way in 1532 in his translation of Plutarch's *Education or Bringeing vp of Children*: "The chiefe or capitayne of them was named Polyphemus, who excelled al the other in enormitie of stature."[21]

Polyphemus was the Cyclops who so delighted in eating Odysseus's men in the *Odyssey*, as those of you who suffered Cyclops-related nightmares from being read this book as a child may recall. Given that he was exceedingly large, wicked, and abnormal looking, it is possible that Elyot could have been using the word to mean any of these three possible meanings. But since he refers specifically to the "enormitie of stature," it is most likely that the word refers to the Cyclops's great size.

So it would appear that these two senses of enormity are both hundreds of years old. Why are people still so exercised about this one meaning? In large part because it is perceived to be nothing more than a mistake. But if this word, which has been in fairly common use for hundreds of years, is a mistake, then so are our uses of many other beloved *enorm-* words.

After all, *enormous* did not used to mean "enormous"—at least not the sense of it that we use today. The first known use of *enormous* was to mean "deviating from the norm, typically in a bad sense." And *enormousness* (which is sometimes recommended as "the word you use instead of *enormity* when you want to refer to something that is very large") had the singular meaning of "great wickedness" for the first two hundred years it was in use (from the early seventeenth to the early nineteenth century).

It is unlikely that anyone who has refused to accept the "new" meaning of *enormity* will be swayed now by these observations. Some people have been misusing this word for hundreds of years and other people have been telling them to not do it for almost as long; such things do not change easily. The abuse of language and the abuse of people who do so are both part of the human condition.

It is also part of the human condition to be patently illogical regarding which new meanings of old words we accept and which we resist. But I have a theory that makes it seem almost logical. We are looking for two things when we accept new meaning in an existing word: It must stand for a concrete action or thing, and its use must represent a dramatic shift in meaning.

For an example of a word that has changed meaning and done so in a way that meets both of these criteria we need look no further than our desks. For an excellent example is provided by the small auxiliary device that has been responsible for introducing untold numbers of people to the words *carpal* and *tunnel*: the computer mouse.

We all know what a computer mouse is. Use of this recent technological addition is widespread—you may be using one right now to scroll down this page—and it is likely that we have all used the word *mouse* to refer to it, without worrying much that we were doing anything unseemly to the English language. The main confusion with this word has been about whether it is proper to refer to them in the plural as *mice* or *mouses*. We have all accepted this word. If the person sitting in the next cubicle at work suddenly insisted that it was not a *mouse* that you used to navigate with on your screen, because *mouse* had referred to one of the smaller specimens of the family Muridae for a thousand years, and he was instead going to refer to it as an "x-y position indicator for a display system," because that was how Douglas C. Englebart (the inventor of the device) referred to it in his patent filing,* you would likely find yourself another cubicle to sit in.

The computer *mouse* represents a concrete thing, and that thing is not closely related to the original meaning of the word (at least not so close that people would confuse them). Numerous other bits of computer language are likewise concrete and disassociated from their original meaning and have been smoothly accepted as decent English. We open a new *window* in a *web browser*, click on an *icon*, and so forth—all these words have recently taken on new semantic content in a manner that is far removed from previous meanings.

By contrast, there are other computer-related words that are open to complaint and peevery, and this happens especially if the

----

* The patent number is US 3541541 A, awarded on November 17, 1970.

new meaning is too closely related to the old. For many people, the introduction of the words *friend* (as a verb, meaning to indicate some sort of overture of friendship via electronic communication, or a noun, indicating someone with whom you have exchanged social media fluids) and *like* (meaning, loosely, to like something, but perhaps not enough to do anything about it beyond clicking on a button on a computer screen) provoke rage. These words are too close to what people commonly think of as their original meanings.

Perhaps this is what happened with *enormity*: It shifted its meaning, but it did not shift it *enough*. Had some Silicon Valley titan but come up with a new device for the computer that was then seized by millions of frantically thumb-typing young people, who then decided to call it an *enormity*, it might have escaped such censure.

In short, we are open to semantic inventiveness and resistant to semantic drift. The former represents a healthy form of ingenuity; an old word repackaged and applied to some new invention. The latter reminds us of something that is inexorably and gradually slipping away; our lost youth and vigor, as represented by the immutable mutability of language.

ENERVATE

Contrary to what many people think, the verb *enervate* does not mean "to invigorate, energize."

—*American Heritage Dictionary Define-a-thon for the High School Freshman, 2007*

> As I left the hall, agitated and enervated, I remember chuck-
> ling to myself, with great satisfaction, "I have done it—I have
> done it."
>
> —John Bartholomew Gough, *An Autobiography*, 1845

If you are one of those people who regularly misuse *enervate*, pat yourself on the back, for you are in highly educated company. An article in the *Atlantic Monthly* from 1934, written by noted vocabulary expert Johnson O'Connor, reported that 52 percent of college graduates surveyed believed incorrectly that *enervating* meant "invigorating," while only 16 percent chose the correct definition of "weakening."[22] I do not believe that any recent surveys have taken stock of whether the college graduates of today are less likely to confuse the two, but it seems unlikely that our vocabulary skills have improved over the past eight decades.

An explanation sometimes offered as a way to remember the difference between such similar words is that *enervate* comes from the Latin word *enervare*, meaning "to cut the sinews out" (which was the original meaning of *enervate* in English), whereas *energize* comes from a Greek word *energeia*, meaning "activity." However, this kind of trick, based on remembering the meaning of words based on their etymology, is fraught with difficulty, as the users of it run the risk of falling into the bottomless pit of despair mentioned earlier in this chapter, the Etymological Fallacy. Should you rely too heavily on such a trick you are likely to think that *superciliousness* has something to do with eyebrows.*

While it is indisputable that equating *enervating* with *invigorat-*

----

* It comes from the Latin *supercilium*, which means "eyebrow," in addition to "haughtiness."

ing is a mistake, it does seem odd that dictionaries should refuse to acknowledge this split meaning of the word. After all, it would hardly be the first meaning of a word to enter the English language as a mistake. Dictionaries have typically not turned their noses up at words that are born of the incompetence of the language's speakers.

Most dictionaries today tend to view their role as that of recorder of language, rather than watchdog. If enough people use a word in a certain fashion, whether rightly or wrongly, then lexicographers will dutifully note this usage. *Cocoa* is universally accepted in dictionaries as referring to "a powdered form of the ground cacao bean used to make chocolate," yet it is nothing more than a poor spelling of *cacao* that somewhere along the line managed to be misspelled by enough people to gain legitimacy.

The word *internecine* is a fine example of how meanings can change as a result of a simple mistake. It had bounced along happily for about a hundred years, beginning in 1642,* meaning nothing more than "characterized by enormous bloodshed or slaughter." And then that butcher of the English language Samuel Johnson got his filthy paws on it and added a new meaning.

According to *Webster's Dictionary of English Usage,* Johnson mistakenly believed that the Latin prefix *inter-* in this case meant "mutual" and so defined the word in the first edition of his dictionary as "endeavouring mutual destruction." Johnson's dictionary was enormously influential (not in the original sense of *enormously,* which was "criminally") and widely plagiarized by subsequent lexicographers who didn't bother with checking

----

* It is first found in James Cranford's *Teares of Ireland:* "what internecine wars were stirred up against the Hussites in Bohemia?"

whether his entries were correct or not. In no time at all, a new sense of *internecine* was being used, quickly becoming the dominant form; it is exceedingly rare to see anyone today using it in its original sense.

Has this word, born of an obvious mistake, elicited howls of protest? None at all. This may partly be due to the fact that few people, whether they care to defend the English language or not, know what *internecine* means; it is a fairly obscure word.

Fruition likewise had a single meaning in English for several hundred years; it meant "enjoyment; the act of enjoying something" from the beginning of the fifteenth century until the twentieth. At the end of the nineteenth century, however, some language philistines confusedly assumed that it must have something to do with the ripening of fruit and began to use it in the sense of "to come to a desired result." Use of *fruition* in this secondary sense now far outstrips its use in the former sense. You might see such use castigated if you are in the habit of reading early-twentieth-century dictionaries or language guides, but it otherwise appears to have settled into the language without notice.

Spitting image is a common phrase, indicating an exact likeness. It is sometimes found in the variant form *splitting image,* and one will often hear that this is wrong. But if *splitting image* is wrong then so is *spitting image* since both are corruptions of the original phrase, which was *spit and image.*

Spit, in the nineteenth century, commonly meant "likeness," and the phrase *spit and image* is found in use from 1847,* well

----

* In Horatio Moore's *Fitzgerald and Hopkins*: "Oh, it's the very spit and image of my own baby! As like my little baby as two peas!"

before *spitting image* entered the language. *Spit and image* was soon corrupted to *spitten* image, and from there became *spitting image*. So *splitting image* is but another in a long line of increasingly changed versions of an original phrase that no one uses anymore.

None of this should be taken as a plea to elevate the secondary sense of *enervating* to the grand pantheon of Standard English usage. It is not even a plea to put the word into the dictionary with a warning label attached to its ear. It is, however, a plea to restrain yourself from spitting with contempt the next time you encounter someone who uses it in this awkward fashion. Unless, of course, you are entirely certain that none of the words that you yourself use has such uncertain parentage, in which case spit away.

AGGRAVATE

The use of "aggravate" as a synonym for anger or irritate is informal and best avoided; the precise meaning is "make worse."
—Philip B. Corbett, *After Deadline* blog, *New York Times*,
July 16, 2013

She was always a good deal of trouble, and I suspect she will reappear when I least want to see her, skirts too long, shy to the point of aggravation, always the injured party, full of recriminations and little hurts and stories I do not want to hear again, at once saddening me and angering me with her vulnerability and ignorance, an apparition all the more insistent for being so long banished.
—Joan Didion, *Slouching Towards Bethlehem*, 1968

Aggravate has been getting under people's skin for a considerable length of time. The careful reader will note that in the preceding sentence I chose not to go for the cheap wordplay, eschewing some version of "*aggravate* has been *aggravating.*" I likewise chose to not employ one of the many fine synonyms that the English language has for *aggravate*. I did so out of an excess of caution, so that the usage police who so decry the newfangled sense of *aggravate* would not call for my head.

I could have said that this issue has been *irritating* them, but the original meaning of *irritate* was "to rouse or provoke a person to action." To say that it has been *bugging* them is certainly no better, as *bug* has been used to describe the aggravating of people since only the mid-twentieth century. *Bug* obviously has a long and distinguished history of other meanings before that.

Could we say that it has been *exasperating* them? We could, but the same people who hold that *aggravate* has a precise meaning of "to make worse" could rightfully point out that the earliest meaning of *exasperate*, found in 1531, is likewise "to make worse." Desiderius Erasmus, in his morbidly titled *A Treatise Perswadynge a Man Patientlye to suffre the Deth of His Frende*, refers to poor Marcus Crassus, who viewed his son's head after it had been stuck on a spike by his enemies: "the more to exasperate and augme(n)t his calamitie."[23]

In case you were unaware of what is wrong with this use of *aggravate*, the quibble is that some people feel it should properly mean "to make worse" and naught else. While it is true that this meaning of *aggravate* has been attached to the word for a considerable length of time (since the late sixteenth century), it is also true that it has had the current "vogue" meaning for almost as long: the lexicographer John Florio included it in his 1598 dictionary as a definition (along with *exasperate* and *irritate*) for the Italian word *essagerare*. The "exacerbate" and "exasperate" senses of the word *aggravate* entered our language at almost the same time.

However, the sense of "to make worse" is recorded *slightly* earlier, so should we simply say, in the interests of fairness, that this meaning is the better one, if only because it has been used thusly for longer? No, we should not.

There are plenty of words that know how to chew gum and walk at the same time and can multitask their way through the language with ease. One pertinent example is the aforementioned *exasperate*, which for several hundred years managed to contain the meanings "to make worse" and "to aggravate" (as well as multiple others), without breaking a sweat (and without anyone complaining about such a loss of specificity).

Additionally, if we are awarding prizes to meanings based on how long they have existed in English, the "make worse" sense of *aggravate* would not have won first place in this semantic footrace. The first known sense of *aggravate* (as a verb) was for the act of weighing something down. This is not surprising, as the word comes to our language from the Latin *aggravāre*, which has much the same meaning. On top of all this, the verb form of *aggravate* does not even represent the first use of the word in English; it existed as an adjective, in an ecclesiastical sense and referred to being threatened with excommunication. So, in conclusion, *nobody* uses the first meaning of *aggravate*, not even the pedants.

If all this befuddles you, and you would like to say that something *aggravates* you without running the risk of having your audience confused as to whether you intended it to mean "makes you worse," "inflames your disease," "accuses you," "weighs you down," "increases your offensiveness," or any one of the other possibilities that the word offers, then I suggest you just go with *irk*—no one complains much about *irk*.

UNIQUE

Anyone who uses the term *very unique* marks herself as one who's not sharp.
—Phyllis Mindell, *How to Say It for Women*, 2001

After the "Jacobite" the great G. B. & the greater L. M. A. did the "Morning Call" in a very unique manner.
—Louisa May Alcott, letter to Alfred Whitman, February 13, 1859

The argument against using *unique* in any sort of a comparative fashion would seem, on its face, to be a sound one. After all, the inherent quality of *unique* is that it designates a singular thing or quality—saying that something is *more unique* is akin to saying that it is *most best.** Unique* being manhandled in this comparative sense sticks in the craw of many, and once you start paying attention to this use you are likely to begin seeing (and hearing) it everywhere. Linguists might call such usage something like "variation in non-scalar absolute adjectives"; many other people would settle for "poor English."

We speakers and writers of English have long been in the habit of seemingly misusing our comparatives and superlatives: We say that something is "more perfect" (or "less perfect"), a choice of words that appears to indicate that the speaker either does not mean what he says or does not know what the word *perfect* means. We write of "the *supremest* being," as though there were other,

---

* Which Ben Jonson, one of our most celebrated writers, did in his writing: "shee has the most best, true, faeminine wit in Rome!"

supreme-but-not-quite-so-supreme beings. Is this modification of this kind of adjective truly as illogical as it appears? The use of *unique* is the most often cited example of committing sacrilege against the gods of comparative and superlative adjectives, so let's look at this word first.

To cover the basic facts of *unique* that are not under debate: We know that the word began to be used in English at the middle of the sixteenth century, adopted from the French word (which was spelled the same way). It came to the French from the Latin word *ūnicus*, meaning "single of its kind." The first sense in which it was used in English was to denote "something of which there is only one," the sense that many people wished it had kept. It remained semantically pure for some time, and little used. Until the nineteenth century it was still largely considered to be a foreign interloper (the lexicographer Henry Todd referred to it as "an affected and useless term of modern times" in his 1818 version of *Johnson's Dictionary*).[24] But when it began to be more widely adopted by writers, later in the nineteenth century, *unique* acquired the disagreeable habit of so many words that enter into common parlance: It began to broaden its meaning.

This is visible in the work of a wide variety of writers. Thomas Burgess, writing in *An Essay on the Study of Antiquities* slays two absolute adjectives in a single sentence, referring to a poem that becomes "more unique and perfect."[25] The poet Walter Scott, writing in the *Edinburgh Review* in 1816, refers to the merits of Jonathan Swift as being "more unique and inimitable than those of any of his contemporaries."[26] And the authors of the supplement to the 1824 edition of the *Encyclopaedia Britannica* wrote "The most unique practice of the Flemish cultivators is the application of liquid manure."[27] I think that even the strictest grammarians would have to admit that this practice sounds most unique.

Although this debasement of *unique* continued throughout the nineteenth century, language watchers did not appear to pay much attention to it until the beginning of the twentieth century. When they did sit up and take notice, there was widespread condemnation of this use, condemnation that continues to this day. In 1906, the Fowler brothers, writing in *The King's English*, laid down what seemed to be a very simple rule: "A thing is unique, or not unique; there are no degrees of uniqueness."[28]

While the Fowlers have doubtlessly had a certain amount of influence on how we write, their advice in this regard was not taken by everyone, as people have continued to try to write about degrees of uniqueness. In spite of this, the insistence that the meaning that many writers give to this word is a thing that does not actually exist continues to this day. In 2010, *The Little Gold Grammar Book* by Brandon Royal averred that "something cannot be somewhat unique, rather unique, quite unique, very unique, or most unique,"[29] a pronouncement that would come as a surprise to the many writers who have modified this word in these ways since the time of the Fowlers.

None of this is to say that if you prize the original meaning of *unique* you will have it ripped from your hands and trampled on by a horde of jeering semantic Bolshevists. Feel free to continue regarding the precise meaning of *unique* as one of the finer aspects of the English language. However, I would advise that if you take the words of Phyllis Mindell to heart (from the quote at the beginning of this entry) and view "anyone who uses the term *very unique* marks herself as one who's not sharp" you will find yourself living in a world largely populated with people who are not very sharp.

For such modified use of this word is exceedingly common; the examples I have provided are not simply cherry-picked anomalies. Further evidence of this use may be found in modern dictionaries, all of which give a broadened meaning for *unique* in addition to the "singular" one.

The *New Oxford American Dictionary* gives a definition of "particularly remarkable, special, or unusual."[30] The most recent edition of the *Merriam-Webster Collegiate Dictionary* defines it as "unusual," in addition to the traditional meanings.[31] Longman's online *Dictionary of Contemporary English* gives a definition of "unusually good and special,"[32] and the *American Heritage Dictionary* informs us that one of the word's meanings is "remarkable; extraordinary."[33]

These dictionaries are not staffed with permissive slackers; such books are compiled by exceptionally learned people who spend a good deal of time looking at the English language and trying to create a written record that accurately reflects its use. If there is sufficient evidence that people are using a word in a certain manner, the dictionaries will take note of it and describe this usage. This is not to say that they will just write down any form of usage that is in vogue or overheard in the lunchroom; the words must have shown a prolonged use among what is generally considered to be the educated population.

These dictionaries will also often give warnings to uses of words that are considered substandard or that are viewed as problematic. Most of the dictionaries I cited do provide a warning after this broadened definition of *unique*. The *New Oxford American* notes that in the nonabsolute sense *unique* should be used "sparingly." The *American Heritage* takes pains to say that its usage panel disapproves of this use (somewhat less stridently than they once did), although it allows that "the nontraditional modification of *unique* may be found in the work of many reputable writers and has certainly been put to effective use," before giving examples of such use by Martin Luther King Jr. and science journalist Natalie Angier. The entry in *Merriam-Webster's Collegiate* states that "in modern use both comparison and modification are widespread and standard," although they stress that when the word is used in its traditional sense "*unique* is used without modifiers."

Do we have any rhyme or reason to how we modify *unique*? Yes, we do, and the way we do so is fairly clear. When we modify *unique*, the tendency is to do so with an auxiliary word, rather than a prefix. The phrase "more unique" is fairly common: Charlotte Brontë, in the preface to *Jane Eyre*, wrote "I have alluded to him, Reader, because I think I see in him an intellect profounder and more unique than his contemporaries have yet recognized."[34] And in a letter to Harriet Moore from January 31, 1915, Ezra Pound wrote "I assure you it is better, 'more unique,' than the other poems of Eliot which I have seen."[35] Yet the use of *uniquer* is exceedingly rare. It is practically nonexistent, save when used jocularly to indicate that the speaker is poorly educated.

The use of *uniquest* is not quite as rare as *uniquer*; Horace Walpole used this questionable superlative in a letter to Horace Mann in 1772: "I have changed all my Roman medals of great brass, some of which were very fine, particularly a medaliuncino of Alexander Severus, which is unique, far the *uniquest* thing in the world; a silver bell for an inkstand, made by Benvenuto Cellini."[36] And the nineteenth-century poet Francis Turner Palgrave described the later work of Shelley as his "very finest, uniquest, most magically delightful work."[37] But although *uniquest* makes an occasional appearance, it is far more likely that "most unique" will be used.

Oddly enough, one of the earliest uses of *unique* in any form may be found in a 1553 work by Gawin Douglas, *The XIII Bukes of Eneados of the Famose Poete Virgill*, which contains the line "Nor yit

Achilles chare, persauis draw Thocht athir *vniquest* the in feild,
we knaw."[38] However, this book was a translation from Latin into
the Middle Scots tongue, so we should not view it as evidence that
uniquest has some great lineage in English.

Nor is the modification of *unique* merely the habit of long-dead
writers and modern-day illiterates. George Orwell referred to
Dickens as "almost unique,"[39] and Christopher Hitchens wrote of
"the idea that this made the terrestrial globe much more unique."[40]

The sordid history of *unique* represents an extreme example,
but it is far from the only adjective that has been deemed incapable of being modified. These improper adjectives that most
often offend grammarians tend to be the ones that also indicate
some ultimate quality. *Perfect* represents a fine example, so when
Claudio says "Silence is the perfectest herald of joy" in *Much Ado
About Nothing*, or Lady Macbeth refers to a "perfectest retort" we
may imagine that people rent their garments in despair. Or at
least they would have, had it not been Shakespeare who wrote
these lines, since people today generally give him a pass on such
misuse of language.

It is notable that writers and editors have not always been content to grant Shakespeare leniency in these matters. Alexander
Pope, in editing the Bard's works, was prone to removing double
superlatives (as well as other instances of questionable syntax). In
Julius Caesar, Pope changed the immortal line "this was the most
unkindest cut of all" to the somewhat blander "This, this, was the
unkindest cut of all," rendering Antony grammatically correct but
removing some of the essence of the line. In the same play, Pope
changed "With the most boldest, and best hearts of Rome" to
"With the most bold, and the best hearts of Rome."[41]

The problem with the double superlative (the word *most* followed by an -*est* word) is that is it viewed as illogical. People who

use them are attempting to modify something that by definition cannot be modified. These are words that represent some quality that either *is* or *isn't*—there is no wiggle room. Or is there?

Adjectives, those oft-maligned modifiers of nouns, may be gradable or non-gradable. A gradable adjective refers to something that can have a shifting degree of quantity. For instance, a man may be as *dumb* as you, he may be *dumber* than you, or he may be the *dumbest* person you have ever met. These are all examples of a gradable adjective. However, should he be *dead*, that is a condition that would allow no wiggle room; he cannot be *more dead*, no matter how much you might wish him so. Hence we generally shy away from using the word *deader*, except in colloquial or jocular use (such as "deader than a doorknob").

These non-gradable types are also frequently referred to as absolute adjectives, and it is widely considered improper to attempt to use them in a comparative fashion, despite a large body of evidence indicating their use has been widespread by both noted and not-so-noted users of English. For instance, *pregnant* is something that one is or is not—you cannot be partially pregnant. However, the word is still often used in a gradable sense, indicating how far along in a pregnancy a woman is. One might refer to a woman who is in the end of her final trimester as "very pregnant," a situation in which *pregnant* refers to something more specific than just meaning "with child."

It is easy to see how a word such as *pregnant* might take on additional shades of meaning since we use it already in a variety of other settings (such as the phrase "a pregnant pause"). But it becomes more difficult to defend the use of other absolute adjectives when their meaning is widely understood to amount to the ultimate version of something. A fine example of such misuse can be found in the preamble of the U.S. Constitution, that document that is beloved by so many and read by so few. The first line begins with "We the People of the United States," which is all well and good, so far as the grammarians are concerned, but quickly falls apart after that, as the founders of our nation then wrote "in Order to form a more perfect Union." If we follow the reasoning that absolute adjectives should not, nay, cannot be modified, then "more perfect" is a rather large blunder. After all, something is either *perfect* or it is not.

The solution to this may be found by investigating the miscreant adverbs *more* and *most*. These words have not always functioned simply as comparatives and superlatives. They also, for much of the history of English, have served as intensifiers. We see this often in sentences such as "I had a most interesting evening." When we use it this way we are not saying "the evening I had was the most interesting evening ever"; we are simply saying that it was "quite interesting."

There are very few, if any, absolute adjectives that people have not tried to modify at one time or another. It appears to be an irresistible habit. Doubtless this is in large part due to people being lax with their language use, but on other occasions it simply represents a desire to be more emphatic. In the eighteenth century the grammarian Robert Lowth railed against the modification of absolute adjectives, but considered the phrase "most highest" entirely acceptable. *Perfect* has likewise been pushed and prodded by careful and careless users of English. In addition to the "more perfect" found in the Constitution, *less perfect* is a fairly common turn of phrase (even though it, too, assumes that there can be degrees of perfection), showing up in the writings of Karl Popper,[42] Isaac Newton,[43] Charles Darwin,[44] and hundreds of others.

A number of eighteenth-century grammarians in addition to

Lowth complained about this habit of trying to make an adjective into something that it was not. The grammarian Lindley Murray inveighed against such sloppiness in using *perfect* more than two hundred years ago, stating "The phrases *more perfect*, and *most perfect*, are improper."[45] Once again, this sounds quite reasonable, and had the grammarians focused their efforts on a small group of words that really bothered them perhaps they would have had more success in stemming the tide of graded absolute adjectives (although probably not). But these guardians of our language began to compile an increasingly long list of words that they felt could not be modified. Their insistence that such words as *steady*, *extreme*, and *square* should not be modified in any way failed to find favor with most people.

If there is any reasonable admonishment on the subject to leave you with, it might be this: The inclination to anoint adjectives of any kind absolute can lead to trouble. Once you begin to declare that a word has a rigid meaning you run the risk of having an increasing number of other words appear similarly non-gradable. You start out with noble intentions, seeking no more than to rid the world of the phrase *less unique*, and before you know it you find yourself sniffing when you see the word *emptier* or *fullest* (after all, something is either empty or not, full or not full). Soon you will be coughing not-so-politely when you hear someone utter the words *almost inevitably* because, as should be clear, something is either inevitable or it is not. No one will pay you any attention, except perhaps to offer you a cough drop.

You will then arm yourself with a copy of Joseph Wright's 1838 *Philosophical Grammar of the English Language*, which comes with a very helpful "list of adjectives which admit of no variation of state." Time will soon find you wandering the streets, dressed in rags and muttering disconsolately to yourself whenever you hear anyone modifying the words *dry, wet, straight, flat, equal, clear, evident, correct, quiet,* or *true* (or any of dozens of other adjectives that Wright said cannot be modified).[46]

Or you could accept that certain words, such as *unique* and *perfect,* are used by some people in a less semantically exact manner than you would yourself employ and hope that they have some other redeeming qualities that make up for this lapse.

If you would like guidance in the regard of how you should use *unique,* Kingsley Amis had some wise, albeit pessimistic words on the matter. He wrote that the habit of using it to simply mean "unusual" "is so notorious among the almost-literate that, like the split infinitive, anything reminiscent of it is best avoided." While Amis allowed that some grades of *unique* might well make sense (such as "rather unique"), "I would not advise anybody to use it who fancies a quiet life."[47]

two

Words That Are Not Words

One of the common myths about how language works is that if there is a seeming need for a word, and if one simply thinks long and hard about it and then comes up with a truly fine candidate, then this neologism will stand a decent chance of being adopted into the language. This almost never happens, outside of the realm of scientific terminology (which is obviously a domain populated by sadists with no regard for language). A rare exception is *scofflaw*, a word with what may be the humblest possible origin story: It was created in order to win a prize in a newspaper contest.

In 1924, a fervent prohibitionist named Delcevare King felt that there was a hole in the heart of the English language, as he saw no word that would adequately describe those who failed to observe the Eighteenth Amendment (which banned the manufacture, transportation, and sale of alcoholic beverages). So King ran a contest, with the extravagant sum of $200 offered to whoever came up with the best name for a person who in any way failed to abide by the terms of this amendment. Some twenty-five thousand would-be word creators wrote in with suggestions, including *sliquor, patrinot*, and *boozshevik*.

The winning entry was *scofflaw*, a rather simplistic blend of two older English words, and it was submitted independently by two people, Henry Dale and Kate Butler. The word quickly took hold, due in large part to the publicity surrounding the contest, which was promoted heavily in the *Boston Globe*.

King tried to continue in this role of *éminence grise* of language, holding additional contests on such subjects as a new slogan for the National Recovery Association. The winner of this contest (awarded the slightly less munificent sum of $10) was "N.R.A. Saves Us," which obviously failed to replicate the success of *scofflaw*. King had had his moment of glory in the furthering of the English language and was forever associated with the word; so much so that when his father, Theophilus King, died in 1935, the obituary announced among his accomplishments that he was the father of the man who gave the world *scofflaw*.

There were many other such contests in the twentieth century, few of which had any success (*skycap*, which was created to come up with a new word for *porter*, was one exception). The Eveready company, makers of flashlights, tried to extend their manufacturing range to language in 1917, when they offered the astonishing prize of $3,000 to whoever could come up with a better word for flashlight. The results of this contest were noteworthy only insofar as Eveready was generous enough to pay the full prize amount to all four of the contestants who sent in the winning word. That word was *day-lo*. It worked out about as well as *sliquor* and *boozshe-*

vik did. Such failed attempts served only to show how difficult it can be to try to force a new word into a language.

Sometimes the urge is not to create a new word to describe a thing for which there is no existing word, but instead to replace a word that is disliked. This has happened more than once for the word *jazz*. The same year that the contest was held to find *scofflaw* a bandleader named Meyer Davis decided that there was a need to replace *jazz*, which he thought had lost its expressiveness. Approximately seven hundred thousand people sent in suggestions in an attempt to win the $100 prize, which was split between two people who sent in the same word. That word, which has utterly failed in its intended goal of replacing *jazz*, was *synco-pep*.

Jazz was subjected to a recall campaign again in 1949, when *DownBeat* magazine called for submissions to replace it, offering $1,000. In the face of stiff competition from words such as *blip* and *jarb*, the word *crewcut* was chosen and went on to have no effect whatsoever upon the language.

The success of *scofflaw* notwithstanding, it remains true that it is exceedingly unlikely that you, or anyone you know, will ever be able to create a word and see it have widespread use; that just isn't how language works. Although we do frequently see words introduced into the language (such as *blog, staycation*, and innumerable political scandals ending with the suffix *-gate*), such words usually do not survive for long and are generally not the result of an individual spontaneously deciding to create a word. Even *scofflaw* has not been entirely successful as it began to change its meaning shortly after it was adopted by large numbers of English speakers. The original meaning of "one who does not pay attention to the Eighteenth Amendment" is now entirely obsolete; the word is now used to mean "one who fails to pay his parking tickets; a person who violates the law." What better demonstration of the English language's ineluctable penchant for change: Even when we create a specific word for a specific purpose it refuses to be bound by its origins.

This is not to say that words do not enter the language by invention; they do, and frequently so. Inventive writers, especially those who are widely read, have had notable success in coming up with words that then become part of our language. Lewis Carroll was responsible for *chortle* and *bandersnatch*, found first in *Through the Looking Glass*. Shakespeare invented a large number of words, although not nearly as many as he was credited with (see page 186). James Joyce had numerous coinages (few of which, admittedly, have passed beyond the furrowed brows of graduate students), as have Gelett Burgess (*goop*, *blurb*) and Winston Churchill (credited with *seaplane* and *undefendable*).

But these were well-known or renowned authors, and we tend to give wide latitude to such creatures. When new words of less illustrious parentage come around, they typically are met far less welcomingly. If you have pinned your hopes on being long remembered for having contributed some sparkling gem that enriches the English language, you are setting yourself up for disappointment.

The words in this chapter have all been introduced, or reintroduced, to the English language in the last several hundred years. All of them were at some point widely scorned; they have seen varying degrees of acceptance since their introduction. The fact that these words, each of which has been labeled at some point "not a word," remain in use illustrates that prognosticating about the future of our language is often a fool's game.

BELITTLE

> [Belittle] has no chance of becoming English; and, as the more critical writers of America, like all those of Great Britain, feel no need of it, the sooner it is abandoned to the incurably vulgar, the better.
>
> —Fitzedward Hall,
> *Recent Exemplifications of False Philology,* 1872

> We will not belittle them, but they were the trials of mind and spirit working in calm surroundings, often beyond even the sound of the cannonade.
>
> —Winston S. Churchill, *Marlborough,*
> *His Life and Times, Book One,* 1933

Chances are very good that when you use the word *belittle* you do not pause immediately after, worriedly checking to see if anyone in the room has noticed the grave faux pas you've just committed. Well, you should. If you are American, you should feel a deep and abiding sense of shame for having shown your true rustic character. And if you are British you should feel an even deeper sense of shame for having uttered such an impossibly yokelish word. At least, that's what some people would have thought in the eighteenth century.

Belittle may look like a fine old English word, but it has the whiff of cheap backwoods neologism to it. It was coined in the early 1780s by Thomas Jefferson, shortly after the American Revolution; a time when there was a marked tendency on the part of some residents of the United Kingdom to cast aspersions at our country. Jefferson used the word (in the sense "to make small") in *Notes on the State of Virginia*, in response to what he thought were incorrect notions of American wildlife made by Georges-Louis Leclerc, the Comte de Buffon: "So far the Count de Buffon has carried this new theory of the tendency of nature to belittle her productions on this side the Atlantic."[1]

To say that the word was disparaged is an understatement. An article from the *London Review* provides a fine, if slightly melodramatic, example of how the British reacted to Jefferson's coinage: "Belittle!—What an expression!—It may be an elegant one in Virginia, and even perhaps perfectly intelligible; but for our part, all we can do is, to *guess* at its meaning.—For shame, Mr. Jefferson!—Why, after trampling upon the honour of our country, and representing it as little better than a land of barbarism—why, we say, perpetually trample also upon the very grammar of our language, and make that appear as Gothic as, from your description, our manners are rude?—Freely, good sir, we will forgive all your attacks, impotent as they are illiberal, upon our *national character*; but for the future, spare—O spare, we beseech you, our *mother-tongue!*"[2]

Most language commentators did not resort to such hyperbole, but there was a vitriolic reaction to Jefferson's word, which persisted through the nineteenth century. As late as 1926, Fowler's *Dictionary of Modern English Usage* labeled the word an "undesirable alien."[3] Today, needless to say, *belittle* is in wide use on both sides of the Atlantic.

BALDING

There can hardly be a present participle, "balding," unless there is a verb, "to bald," and standard dictionaries give no such word.

—M. P. Johnson, Letter to the *New York Herald Tribune*, May 22, 1952

Bald, v.—Obs. To make bald. Deprive of hair. *lit.* and *fig.*
—*Oxford English Dictionary*, 1st edition, 1933

One of the reasons I have such a healthy skepticism for so many of the rules for and suggestions on the proper use of English is that when you look at many of the rules from a generation or two back, they often appear laughable. Theodore Bernstein's views on the word *balding*, which were not uncommon in the middle of the twentieth century, present an excellent example.

Bernstein was a respected writer on language and English usage. He wrote seven books on the subject, most of which are still in print. Additionally, he was a professor at the school of journalism at Columbia University and served as an editor for the *New York Times* for a number of decades.

He wrote with a fine and clear style and had considerably more wit in his text than one usually finds in usage guides. He also managed to avoid sounding like a pompous ass (a rarity in such works), offering reasonable advice on such matters as splitting infinitives (do so when necessary), putting a preposition at the end of a sentence (do it if it makes the sentence stronger), and using adjectives as nouns (didn't bother him much). In short, he seems like precisely the sort of person to whom we should look for guidance on matters of language use.

But even with someone as levelheaded as Bernstein, it quickly becomes apparent how difficult and impractical it is to create rules to govern our eternally inchoate language. Bernstein greatly disliked the word *balding*, enough so that he attacked it in more than one of his books.

In *The Careful Writer* (1965) he says of *balding*: "There is no need for such a word. Why not baldish?"[4] Feeling the need to revisit the issue and make his point more emphatically, he returns to the subject two years later in *Watch Your Language*, asserting "There is no such word as 'balding,'" adding once again the plaintive-sounding query "Why not 'baldish'?"[5]

Bernstein was not alone in finding *balding* offensive. The first edition of the *American Heritage Dictionary* questioned its usage panel (composed of approximately a hundred writers and scholars of English) on the subject, and although 55 percent responded that they would not prescribe against the word, some respondents were less than enthusiastic about it. Isaac Asimov picked the word up with a tissue and said that it was "distasteful but necessary." Among the minority respondents, there were slightly more emphatic views; Katherine Anne Porter referred to it as "entirely vulgar." The main complaint against *balding* was that it appeared that people were trying to create a participle form of the word *bald*, which, as everyone knows, is not a verb. This was an eminently reasonable argument to make, save for the fact that *bald* was used as a verb in English in the seventeenth century.

A few years after the *American Heritage* examined the *balding* vs. *baldish* conundrum, *Harper's Dictionary of Contemporary Usage* posed the question to their own panel of whether they found *balding* to be offensive or not. Most did not mind it much, but it did have detractors: George Cornish, the editor of the *New York Herald*

Tribune sputtered "Surely no one uses 'balding' except as a joke at the expense of Timestyle."[6] *Time* magazine was known for popularizing a fair number of vogue words (such as *tycoon* and *socialite*) that were found objectionable by many people. They did not actually invent most of these words, although they were often credited with having done so.

In Bernstein's defense, *balding* does appear to have entered common usage only a few decades before he began writing his jeremiads against it. So it may well have seemed like a faddish word, and we may understand his umbrage with it the same way we can understand how someone today might resent having to listen to all the new uses of the words *friend* and *like* that have crept into English as a result of various kinds of social media.

But even if we allow that Bernstein was not simply making up his rules as he went along, this example does illustrate how difficult it is to predict not only which words will stick around in English but also which ones will come to be seen as acceptable. Bernstein also thought (as did many others) that *package*, used to mean *parcel*, was a fad word and advocated for its use only with discretion. *Balding* has become considerably more common than *baldish*. It is in widespread use among careful writers the world over. I am sure that there are still some people who feel that this word is a rank interloper (some of you are perhaps reading this right now, seething in silent rage), but even they must admit that this is a battle that has been lost.

STUPIDER

> One closing grammar note: I got several letters from people who informed me that "stupidest" and "stupider" are not real words. To those people, I say, with gratitude and sincerity: Oh, shut up.
> —Dave Barry, *Washington Post*, January 19, 2003

> Only stupid people use the word "stupider" because they're to (*sic*) pathetic to know it's not a word.
> —post by Internet user Car-Wash Romance on Yahoo answers,
> October 7, 2012

Several years ago I had the opportunity to be interviewed on a number of radio shows, following publication of a book I wrote about reading the *Oxford English Dictionary*, titled (rather unimaginatively) *Reading the OED*. As is often the case when one is answering the same question many times over, I fell into the habit of often repeating certain phrases, one of which was that "I've never come away from reading the dictionary feeling *stupider*, and there are not many activities about which one can make that claim."

After I had made several iterations of this statement I discovered that there were a number of people who were quite unhappy with me for saying it. Angry comments were posted on the radio stations' websites, and numerous snippy emails were sent to me, all of which expressed more or less the same sentiment: "I initially thought you were an interesting and intelligent man, but then I heard you use the word 'stupider' and immediately realized that you are nothing but a fool, and I shall never again listen to anything you have to say on the subject of language."

I must confess to being dumbfounded by these reactions, for two reasons. First, that my use of this word would so inflame the linguistic passions of people that they would take the time to write angry letters and swear undying aversion to anything I had to say on language in the future. Second, I was genuinely unaware that *stupider* belonged to that class of "words that some people think are not real words."

We typically have no problem with saying that someone is smarter, or dumber, than someone else, so why is there such a provision against using the word *stupider*? There are many suggestions for why this use might be considered proper or improper, and unfortunately, none of them is terribly straightforward.

There are a number of rules governing how we modify adjectives. They can be plain or positive (*happy*), comparative (*happier*), or superlative (*happiest*). It all sounds so simple, when you first explain it to a child: if you have an adjective and you want to make it more of that thing you just add an *-er* to the end of it. If you want to make it the greatest example of that quality you just add an *-est* to it. These modifications are referred to as being inflectional: You inflect the word by adding an ending and hope that everyone understands exactly what you mean. Not so fast—there is a veritable cavalcade of rules just waiting to rap you on the knuckles for inflectional adjective abuse.

First of all, there are general exceptions: words such as *good*, *bad*, and *far* do not play by the same rules as the other comparatives and superlatives—they modify themselves with better/best, worse/worst, and farther/farthest.

Adjectives with one syllable almost always work well with adding *-er* or *-est*. Once again, there are exceptions—some words, such as *ill*, typically require the addition of *more* or *most* in front of them.* Also, there is a tricky group of adjectives known as absolute, or non-gradable adjectives. These are words such as dead, wrong, and right, which typically one either is or is not. (See page 35 for more on this subject.) Many non-gradable adjectives take neither -*er*/-*est* nor more/most.

In some cases, two-syllable adjectives can be modified with -*er* and -*est*, and in some cases they cannot—it depends largely on how the word ends. Those that end with a vowel, or a vowel sound (such as *yellow* or *fancy*), tend to be fine with -*er* and -*est*.

Most two-syllable adjectives that end in a consonant reject the -*er* and -*est* endings. It sounds peculiar to our ear to hear words such as *righteouser*; we say "more righteous." But there are a number of these specimens that are fine with becoming single-word comparatives or superlatives: pleasanter/pleasantest, solemner/solemnest, and wicked/wickedest all sound reasonable to most people.

So why did *stupider* receive such a poor usage label? If we were to look at this word as the linguists do (which is to say, with an eye toward simultaneously annoying people and putting them to sleep), we could say that it is a disyllabic (two-syllable) adjective ending with an alveolar stop (the word ends by the speaker touching their tongue to the alveolar ridge, right behind the teeth), and there are plenty of other words that match this description, and which function with -*er* and -*est*. The linguist R. M. W. Dixon examined this subject in minute detail in a paper on comparative adjectives, pointing out that *politer* and *solider* raise few objections, and attributed this to the words having an alveolar stop and also

----

* And there is an exception to this exception: the adjectival *ill*, when found in hip-hop or rap lyrics, uses the comparative and superlative without feeling bad about it. For instance, Gang Starr, in the song "You Know My Steez," released in 1996, raps "I come with mad love and plus the illest warlike tactics."

due to the fact that they are relatively common. Dixon also uses this argument to make the case for *stupider* being widely accepted, which goes to show that one can be linguistically correct, enormously scholarly, and widely ignored.[7]

One frequently hears that adjectives of more than two syllables should not be modified by an -*er*, and should instead have the word *more* in front of them (such modifications are referred to as periphrastic). This seems obvious in cases such as *more preposterous* (which would sound rather silly as *preposterouser*), but like so many rules, it has exceptions. Particularly if you look at adjectives modified by the addition of *un-*, examples such as *uneasier* and *unsightlier* work just fine, even with three or four syllables.

We did not used to be so worried about tacking -*er* and -*est* endings onto words. John Nesfield, in *English Grammar: Past and Present*, notes that Shakespeare was fond of inflecting adjectives in a way that would make a present-day English teacher burble, using honourablest, ancienter, eminentest, famousest, delectablest, and many such others.[8]

Stupider remains verboten for many people, and I have no illusions that the last paragraphs will change their minds. But it does feel rather capricious, particularly when considering that the superlative form of the word occasions hardly any complaints at all. Typically, if an adjective will not take -*er* as a comparative, it will also not take -*est* as a superlative. We do not say that someone is honester than someone else, and so it follows that we would likewise not say "so-and-so is the honestest person I know."* Yet we

----

* Although Lord Chesterfield, who was Samuel Johnson's patron and a noted adherent to careful language use, used this particular superlative: "He who loves himself best is the honestest man."

would have little trouble saying "When you use the word *stupider*, it makes you sound like the stupidest person in the room."

There is, it should be noted, no unanimity of opinion on whether *stupider* is in fact a word that should bring on the dunce's cap for he who utters it. But what is odd about this is that it appears to have been a case of a usage proscription that occurred without any authority having proclaimed it.

I have seen no usage guides condemning *stupider*, and most dictionaries that mention it do so only in providing the comparative and superlative forms of *stupid*. *Harrap's Essential English Dictionary* (published in 1996) lists both *stupider* and *stupidest*, as does the *American Heritage Dictionary* (5th edition). One occasionally finds the word elsewhere, as when the *Chambers Pocket Guide to Good English* (published in 1985) takes pains to remind its readers that *stupider* should not have two *p*'s in it.

These sources are all from the late twentieth century, which might arouse suspicion that what we are witnessing here is nothing more than a parcel of dictionary writers who have thrown up their hands and given up on people ever learning to not use *stupider*. But the word was certainly in use before the 1980s.

Stupider has been in persistent, although not common, use throughout the past four hundred years. It is found first in Thomas Tuke's 1625 *Concerning the Holy Eucharist*: "Wherein y'are stupider then they, then stones."[9] Occasionally it cropped up in the eighteenth century, as in a translation of the poems of Catullus from 1795, which used both the comparative and superlative in one line: "Who stupider far than the stupidest clown, Should dare the sweet measure of numbers explore."[10]

Writers persisted on using *stupider* throughout the nineteenth and into the twentieth centuries. Ezra Pound was fond of the word: It appears both in his poetry and his correspondence (the *OED* cites a letter he wrote to William Carlos Williams: "If you weren't *stupider* than a mud-duck you would know that every kick to bad writing is by that much a help for the good").[11] Some writers, such as George Eliot, employed it as a peculiar use of dialect in their fiction, and Richard Rodgers, who included it in the lyrics to the musical *No Strings* ("If I stood over there and looked my way, What a pitiful sight I'd see. Stupid, stupider, stupidest. This is the declension, Of little declining me"). But in addition to jocular use there have been numerous other writers who simply used it as a word. The great British essayist G. K. Chesterton wrote "The English are stupider and less sensitive than you are," and didn't seem to feel at all squeamish about using the word.[12]

If all of this leaves you feeling somewhat muddled about how you should treat your adjectives, fret not, for it is likely that most people you speak to have no firmer a grasp on this matter than you. In the event that you don't want to overburden yourself with all of the suggestions and exceptions listed here, you can always follow the example of nineteenth-century writer William Henry Maxwell, who in his *Introductory Lessons in English Grammar* specified that the word *stupid* can either be modified by adding *more* or *most* before, or by adding an *-er* or *-est* after. But Maxwell's best advice on how to modify any such word was the following dictum: "There is, however, no general rule for comparing such adjectives. The ear is the best guide."[13]

IRREGARDLESS

> Of course, there are a great many people who are not bound down to the ecclesiastical tenets, but the majority of the fashionable world adhere to the custom irregardless of their personal custom.
>
> —*New York Times*, February 21, 1915

> Like "preventative," "irregardless" is a nonsensical and spurious word.
>
> —Frank O. Colby,
> *The Practical Handbook of Better English*, 1947

It is admittedly difficult to offer much by way of defense to the word *irregardless*. It appears to be a malformed and unlovable creation: a perfectly serviceable word, *regardless*, burdened with the tumor-like and wholly unnecessary *ir-* prefix.

It is, much more so than many nonstandard creations, a word used almost entirely in the province of the unlearned and the annoyingly jocular. But has it no redeeming qualities?

Before diving into the question of whether the correct response to encountering a person using *irregardless* is public flogging, a spiteful chuckle, or some other measure, let us look at the origin of the word. The second part of it, the one that no one complains about, comes from the French *regarder* (meaning "to look at, or regard"). The prefix, the part that everyone likes to complain about, is a bit more difficult to pin down.

Ir- is essentially a variant of the prefix *in-*. This prefix has a small variety of meanings and a slightly larger variety of forms, and this has contributed some confusion to its meaning. The form *in-* is most commonly found, but when placed in front of some

Latin words it becomes either *ig-* (as in *ignoble*), *im-* (as in *impure*), or *ir-* (as in *irrespective*). When we find it in front of some Old French words, *in-* changes to *en-* or *em-* (as *enclasp* or *embark*).

In- has three main meanings, some of which can blend into each other in the same word. It can indicate a negative quality (*innocent* is a modification of the Latin word *nocēre*, meaning "to hurt"). It might have the sense "into, toward, on, within," as is found in verbs such as *inflame*. And *in-* can also function as an intensifier, as in cases such as *inflammable*, which can mean "not capable of being set on fire" and also "very much capable of being set on fire."

It would appear likely that *irregardless* was initially used as a humorous combination of *irrespective* and *regardless*, although Dwight Bolinger, writing in *American Speech* in 1940, suggested that it caught on due to the fact that so many other words beginning with the *ir-* prefix carry with them a suggested meaning of "utterly" or "completely." As *irreparable*, *irresponsible*, and *irremediable* all seem to connote that someone or something is completely incapable of being repaired, responsible, or remedied, the hope is that *irregardless* would carry a similar meaning.[14]

Irregardless is not, as has often been said, a creation of the early twentieth century; it dates back at least to the late eighteenth century. A poem published in the *Charleston City Gazette* from June 23, 1795, contains the line "But death, irregardless of tenderest ties, Resolv'd the good Betty, at length, to bereave." It experienced a lull in use for most of the next fifty years, but for the second half of the nineteenth century it is in somewhat common use across most of the United States.

The most common complaint one hears about this word (and one hears it frequently) is that it "is not a word." This is a curious statement to make since *irregardless* does in fact have what most of us would consider to be necessary components of a word—it is a series of letters arranged in a specific order, frequently used in either speech or writing, and indicating a commonly understood meaning.

One may not *like* this word, but that is a far cry from it not *being* a word. It does not matter how many times you cry out, "That is not a word!," the sentiment will have no greater chance of success than if you stepped into traffic and yelled, "That is not a car!" in hopes of not being run over. *Ir-* may indeed be a tumor, but is there not perhaps a chance that it is a benign one, as opposed to some malignant carcinoma on the body of the English language? After all, there is certainly no shortage of other words that have been created through the addition of a superfluous prefix.

We have *inhabitable* and *habitable*, and no one seems to be terribly bothered by them. For a long time it was common in English to see both *personate* and *impersonate*, meaning much the same thing. And you can use *valuable* and *invaluable* with exceedingly similar meanings, without leading your reader down a rabbit hole of lexical confusion.

If one wished to get one's knickers in a twist over a seemingly superfluous prefix, one would do well to follow the example of the National Fire Protection Association (NFPA), which in the 1920s found that an alarming number of Americans were inclined to think that the *in-* of *inflammable* functioned as an indication that something would not burn, rather than that it would. *Inflammable*, at that point, was considerably more common than *flammable* and had been in use for hundreds of years before the shorter word came along.

A spirited public relations campaign ensued, with the NFPA advocating against the use of *inflammable* in order to better assist

Americans in learning to not set their mattresses on fire. The most surprising thing about this episode is the fact that it was largely successful, as efforts to so regulate the language rarely are able to overcome to stubborn intransigence of common usage.* The NFPA was doubtless aided by the fact that many people found the two words confusing to begin with and so opted for the simpler variant. There is some speculation that the NFPA was influenced in their campaign by Benjamin Whorf, a famed linguist who just happened to have spent the first few decades of his professional career working for the Hartford Fire Insurance Company (as a fire prevention specialist, not as a linguist).

A more recent case of a word that people frequently say is not a word came in 2010, when Sarah Palin, then the candidate for the vice presidency of the United States, used the word *refudiate*. Palin was by no means the first person to blend *refute* and *repudiate*—the earliest instance appears to have been in 1891, when the Fort Worth, Texas, *Gazette* wrote "it is the first declaration of how the party stands, and in great measure a *refudiation* of the charges of dickering."[15]

Refudiate continued to pop up throughout the next century or so, although it always appears to have been used simply as a mistake. Senator Mike DeWine preceded Palin by a few years when he said "Sherrod Brown needs to *refudiate* these comments."[16] After Palin's utterance, and subsequent tweet ("Peaceful Muslims, pls

----

* Although having been successful in managing to elevate *flammable* over *inflammable*, the NFPA now is still faced with the public's ignorance over what *flammable* means. There is apparently a widespread belief that something marked *flammable* is less of a fire hazard than something that is marked *combustible*, which is the opposite of what the NFPA believes (Wogalter et al. 2010).

refudiate"), the use of *refudiate* skyrocketed. Much of its use is what might kindly be referred to as jocular (and unkindly referred to as spiteful).

Yet if *refudiate* overcomes the obstacles of a troubled childhood, pulls itself up by its bootstraps, gets a scholarship to a good school, takes a low-paid position at a company, and ends up marrying the daughter (or son) of the president of that company, it wouldn't be the first such word to do so, or even the first word used by a politician. Warren Harding was brutally mocked for his use of the word *normalcy* in the presidential campaign of 1920—the word was widely, and mistakenly, believed to be a mistaken form of *normality*. After all the excitement died down* *normalcy* managed to take on all the trappings of respectability, and hardly anyone pays it much attention these days.

For those of you who fail to be swayed by arguments in favor of accepting that this upstart is a word of any kind and who continue to rage against the unwashed masses who insist on using it, you may at least take comfort in knowing that *irregardless* is not the worst possible form of this word. In an 1887 book by Emilie Lancaster, *'Tween Heaven and Earth*, we are introduced to the character Sybil Featherstone (the "only daughter of a retired guano merchant") thusly: "She is not disposed to wed whom society and the wise in the world allot to her unregardless."[17]

----

* In 1920, the *Kansas City Star* wrote: "We have the impression the word 'normalcy' would cause a shudder to disturb a professorial frame in the Democratic camp. Cabinet members have been dismissed for less."

three

Verbing Nouns

Imagine the person who utters or writes the following sentence: "We will *liaise* with you, and in order to *optimize* and *impact* our returns, will seek to *incentivize* things with a truly great offer." You might have trouble envisioning the author of that sentence, as you are too busy clawing your eyes from your head, aghast as you are at the four horrific verbed nouns contained within.[*]

It is easy to find fault with this rather egregious example, but it is also worth questioning whether the practice of prescribing against making verbs of nouns (and its obverse, making nouns of verbs) has a metaphoric leg to stand on. Consider the following

----

[*] A verbed noun, also referred to as a "verbal," is an example of a noun that has been coerced into living its life as a verb. In the sentence "I am going to shop at a shop" the first *shop* is a verbed noun, and the second one is, obviously, simply a noun.

sentence: "Many people in our land gripe incessantly about what they find to be the foulest plague to ever visit our language of English: verbing a noun." The preceding sentence contains seven nouns, five of which also commonly function as verbs, and five verbs, of which four commonly function as nouns. Yet these instances are far less likely to make language lovers feel itchy with frustration than are such cases as *liaise* and *impact*. Why is this?

One simple explanation is that the use of *liaise* and *impact* as verbs is fairly recent (they date more or less from the middle of the twentieth century). Another reason is that these words are common forms of business jargon, and we all love to make fun of the way that businesspeople use language.

Additionally, some people have a suspicion that the verbing of nouns is peculiar to American speech or writing and, as such, somehow represents the continuing decline of English. It is a common practice in Great Britain to bemoan the pernicious influence that we Americans have had upon our mutual language. Language watchers on the other side of the Atlantic declare that we upstarts have been sending our infected language to the pristine shores of the United Kingdom, where it then debases their noble speech. "Just have a little taste," our verbed nouns murmur silkily, offering them a free sample just to get them started, much as the apocryphal drug dealer does with an innocent. Once they've had a taste of our linguistic heroin, they want more and more, until soon they are selling their babies, just to buy some more of these dishonored nouns.

The verbed noun arouses special ire in the hearts of the British guardians of English. A recent issue of the *BBC News Styleguide* includes an entire chapter devoted to Americanisms. In it, they warn specifically against these creatures, giving the following sentence as exemplar: "Lambs can be euthanised, he says, but who would care for damaged human children?"[1] The author of the guide, John Allen, then notes, "This sentence was written by a news correspondent in Washington, and illustrates the American enthusiasm for turning nouns into verbs." (*Euthanise* is a verbal formed from the noun *euthanasia*.) Allen points out that although English is not "averse to the practice," engaging in it runs the risk of alienating people. He then launches into the ringing condemnation "*Euthanise* is not a verb you will find in any dictionary and it has no place in our output."

There are two reasons this is a peculiar sentence to have chosen as a means of illustrating an American habit of using a word that "you will not find in any dictionary." First, its use appears to have originated in Great Britain. Second, the word is quite easy to find in numerous dictionaries. Although the author is technically correct: The word is spelled *euthanize*.

The first citation found for *euthanize* in the *Oxford English Dictionary* comes (*quelle horreur!*) from the *Times* of London (that noted embracer of all aberrant American usage), in 1931. The BBC guide is correct in saying that the use of this word as a transitive verb, as opposed to an intransitive one, appears to have originated in North America, but that does not provide such a rousing battle cry ("The Americans are coming, and they're verbing nouns in a transitive manner as they go!"). However, the first attempt to turn the lovely noun *euthanasia* into an unlovely verb of any kind was done in England, with *euthanatize* appearing in the London *Spectator* in 1873.

An additional nine examples of verbed nouns are given by the BBC guide: *author, guest, diarise, civilianize, casualise, finalise, editorialise, miniaturise,* and *publicise.* Combined with the aforementioned *euthanize*, this gives us a nice even ten cases of what supposedly represents an "American enthusiasm."

Of these ten cases, three originated in America: *author* (meaning "to write a book"), *editorialize*, and *miniaturize*. The remaining seven examples were all used first in Great Britain. So if we are to use the examples provided by the BBC, the habit of turning nouns into verbs is hardly the exclusive province of America.

Residents of Great Britain may have a sneaking suspicion that we Americans are responsible for this insidious practice, but it has quite obviously been part of the English language since hundreds of years before the concept of the United States was a mote in the eye of George III. If you attempted to keep your speech clear of any verbs that formerly were nouns you would be rendered unintelligible.

Yet there remains a widespread feeling that this is, at best, an ungainly way to form words. Let us look at some of the verbed nouns that best tickle our angry bone.

IMPACT

And I don't know how many times executives incorrectly use the word "impact." Impact is not a verb.
—Marcia Heroux Pounds,
South Florida Sun-Sentinel, August 30, 2001

Office Depot's third-quarter results were negatively impacted by housing-related economic conditions in key markets, particularly Florida and California, which accounted for 28 percent of North American sales in that period, the company said.
—Marcia Heroux Pounds,
McClatchy-Tribune Business News, December 12, 2007

A considerable body of work is devoted to restraining us from using *impact* as a verb. Usage guides warn, with varying degrees of hysteria, about what people will think of you, should you put together such barbarous collocations as "impact on," "we will impact," and "he impacted the hell outta that ball." Some guides state boldly that "impact is not a verb," while others content themselves with saying something along the lines of "impact is sometimes used as a verb, but it shouldn't be."

The reasoning here is that *impact* functions properly as a noun: One has an *impact on* something, one does not *impact it*. To use it as a verb makes no more sense than to try to use it as an adjective ("it is with an impact heart that I write these words . . ."). However, one small point is oft-overlooked in this continuing fight against the use of *impact* as a verb: it has existed as a verb for much longer than it has as a noun.

The verb form of *impact* has been in use since at least 1601, where it is found in surgical literature, generally to describe problems with the bowels (I'll spare you the full details). And the earliest instance of *impact* in the written record of English isn't a verb or a noun; it has been used since 1563 as an adjective, to indicate that something has been *impacted*. This is good evidence that the word also existed as a verb since as early as the sixteenth century.

What about the noun? The noun, I am sorry to say, is a Johnny-come-lately, although by *lately* I mean "the end of the eighteenth century." The use of *impact* to designate either "an effect had upon something" or "a collision" begins almost two hundred years after the verb had entered our language.

Putting aside for a moment the word's lineage, the complaint against "to impact" is largely with the way it is used. The non-verb crowd feels that using *impact* in a figurative sense (which would appear to be for anything not related to bowels or teeth) is incorrect. This is all well and good, but to claim that it is not a verb, is, to put it mildly, sheer nonsense.

The imbroglio over *impact* is similar to the outcry raised over numerous other examples of long-standing verbs that have recently become popular. *Gift* has been a verb meaning "to endow" for more than four hundred years and has been used for "to give a gift to" for almost as long, but that did not stop Jack Knox, a columnist for the *Prince George Citizen* from calling for capital punishment for anyone who tried to use it as this part of speech.[2]

Many people likewise find fault with using *friend* in the sense of "accepting the electronic invitation of someone in a social media context." Appearing on the ABC news program *Roundtable* in 2012, George Will said that Facebook "has to answer for turning a good serviceable noun, *friend*, into a verb."[3] Poor *friend* was included in the 2010 List of Banished Words, a perennial screed published by the Lake Superior State University, which consists of the words and phrases in English thought most deserving of censure.

What is wrong with *friend* used in this manner? It is easily understood and has obviously been adopted with gusto. It describes an exceptionally old practice (making a friendly acquaintance) that is being pursued in a very modern setting (staring at a screen, removed from actual human contact). Notably absent in the complaints about this word are any viable suggested alternatives.

Friend has been used as a verb for about eight hundred years now, although *befriend* has always been more common. But *be*-prefixed words are on a decline in English (although words such as *bewhiskered* and *bespattered* still have some currency), and there is little likelihood of reversing this trend.

I should point out that while we're in the habit of soldering new meanings onto old language, the *be-* prefix offers some fine opportunities for people who like to be irked about language. Several of the obsolete words formed with *be-* that are documented in the *OED* carry the meaning of "pestering" or "afflicting": *bestench* is defined as "to afflict with stench"; *bemissionary* is "to pester with missionaries"; *bepaper* is "to cover or pester with papers." You could use an imaginary word such as *beverb* to denote the act of "pestering or afflicting with verbs."

FINALIZE

> To use words like "finalize" is merely to be inelegant and to uglify the language.
>
> —Laurence Lafore, in *Harper's Dictionary of Contemporary Usage*, 1985

> Aramintha had flown in from Rome to finalize her divorce, having a month before surprised Giovanni in bed with the bellboy and screwed a broken Fanta bottle into his startled face.
>
> —Martin Amis, *Dead Babies*, 1975

Finalize, in the sense of "to conclude something" is a fairly recent addition to the canon of words that offend people's ears. According to the *Merriam-Webster Dictionary of English Usage*, British writers began to take notice of the offending word in the 1940s, while Americans waited until it was uttered by President Eisenhower in 1958, at which point they too decided that it was worthy of condemnation.

Much ink has been spilled on the subject of how *finalize* came to invade our language. Some have accused Eisenhower of having

introduced it; he obviously didn't, and he also managed to receive unfair treatment for his pronunciation of "nuclear" as *nukular*.*
Here we once again see the common practice among residents of the United Kingdom, when encountering a word that they find detestable, to immediately assume that it must be the Americans' fault.

But *finalize* was in common use in New Zealand and Australia since the early twentieth century, primarily occurring in business writing. It apparently came to America courtesy of the U.S. Navy and shortly after began to be used here in business writing as well.

Although most dictionaries record *finalize* as having entered the language in the early 1900s, the word can be found in occasional use before that. It makes an appearance in a London newspaper, the *Public Advertiser*, in 1780, with a meaning very similar to the one the word has today: "this Bill, at least as it now stands, will perpetuate, not finalize, the Pangs of Adversity."[4]

The word crops up occasionally in the nineteenth century as well—in "The Order of Words in Anglo-Saxon Prose," by C. Alphonso Smith, published in 1893, we find *finalize* used in a linguistic sense: "In O. and W. [Voyages of Ohthere and Wulfstan] the tendency is to finalize, but 4 of the 5 compound temporal clauses have an aux. + verb instead of verb + aux."[5]

None of these uses bothered anyone very much, either because they happened so rarely or because they happened far away. But

----

* Variant pronunciations of nuclear have been common among U.S. presidents, with Jimmy Carter, Bill Clinton, and George W. Bush all eschewing the traditional correct form of *'nü-klē-ər*.

by the middle of the twentieth century *finalize* was one of the most frequently maligned words in the language. The *New York Times* repeatedly poked fun at its use in the 1960s, conveniently overlooking the fact that the word had seen frequent use in their own pages for the past several decades.

The argument most frequently heard against *finalize* is that it is some sort of jargon, a word that would feel more comfortable in a business memo than in a literary missive. Yet some form of this verb is employed in the *Oxford Dictionary of National Biography*, which is as unbusiness-like a book as you could find, no fewer than 150 times.

The suffix *-ize* is one of the most widely disliked in our language, as a result of having shown itself to be remarkably talented at attaching itself to old and respected words and creating new and disrespected ones. Even H. L. Mencken, who did not often find himself on the same side of the barricades as the prescriptivists, hated some *-ize* endings. Of particular irritation to him was the word *obituarize* (meaning "to write an obituary for"). After finding the offending word in a prominent London newspaper, Mencken wrote "If I may intrude my private feelings into a learned work I venture to add that seeing a monster so suggestive of American barbarisms in the *Times* affected me like seeing an archbishop wink at a loose woman."[6]

You may scoff at *incentivize, positivize, obituarize,* and their kin all you like, and these words will find few defenders. I've no quibble with you if you do, so long as you remember that these hated words were born of the same parents as *memorize* and *summarize*.

CONTACT

> The dinner itself was chatter about a jumble of places, person-
> alities, plans, most of which had nothing to do with anything
> that Clyde had personally contacted here.
> —Theodore Dreiser, *An American Tragedy*, 1925

> Dreiser should not be allowed to corrupt his language by writ-
> ing "anything that Clyde had personally contacted here."
> —Review in *The Spectator*, August 6, 1927

The mystery writer Rex Stout was in the habit of having his great
protagonist, Nero Wolfe, act out some of his own strident objections to the misuse of the English language. In *Black Orchids*, Wolfe
says, "Contact is not a verb under this roof."[7] This was the same
character who stood in for Stout in the novel *Gambit*, passing judgment on language use and amusing himself by sitting in front of
a fire and ripping pages out of *Webster's Third New International
Dictionary*, feeding them to the flames. There are a good number
of people (although fewer now than fifty years ago) who still view
using *contact* as a verb of any sort as problematic.

Some people who abhor this word will allow that it can function as a verb, but only a certain kind of verb. *Contact* has long
been thought to have originated as a technical term of the nineteenth century, but it did make occasional appearances in English
well before that. It appears in a 1604 work published by the Church
of England, in a section dealing with the regulation of marriage:
"No persons shall marrie within the degrees prohibited by the
Lawes of God and expressed in a Table set forth by authoritie in
the yeere of our Lord God 1563, and all marriages so made &
contacted shall be adjudged incestuous and unlawfull."[8]

This use is not one of the ones that has been deprecated, in some part because it never became common, or it is simply a misspelling of *contracted*. The verb form of *contact* was in use throughout the eighteenth century, with the meaning "to touch." In 1706, it appears in an anonymous book, *Poems on the Four Last Things*: "the smallest Part with Fire contacted gives excessive Smart."[9] *Contact* continued to appear as a verb in the nineteenth century, generally in a technical sense, referring to such things as gunpowder or electricity coming into contact with something else. No one paid the word much mind.

But then we Americans got our hands on the word and began to use it in an entirely inappropriate manner, referring to the practice of initiating communication with a person. After this all hell broke loose. Well, not quite, but a number of people became upset.

The quote from the *Spectator* at the beginning of this entry is currently the first citation for the word in the *OED*, illustrating a sense that this dictionary defines as "To get into contact or in touch with (a person). orig. *U.S. colloq.*" Three of the first four citations in the *OED* for this sense are from British writers sneering at the American use.

The chances that Dreiser was the first American to use *contact* in the sense of "to contact a person" are slim; more likely his use of it reflects the fact that the word had some currency in speech or writing in America at the time. He was, however, the first one to be censured to it.

The word was apparently given a healthy diet and grew considerably over the next few years, as but six years after Dreiser's use of it in *An American Tragedy* the use of *contact* was memorably decried by an executive of the Western Union Telegraph Company. That man, Frederick W. Lienau, wrote a letter to the managers of the company, making clear his displeasure with the use of the word: "Somewhere there cumbers this fair earth with his loathsome presence a man who, for the common good, should have been destroyed in early childhood. He is the originator of the hideous vulgarism of using 'contact' as a verb. So long as we can meet, get in touch with, make the acquaintance of, be introduced to, call on, interview or talk to people, there can be no apology for 'contact.'"[10]

While it is hard to not admire Lienau's rhetorical flourishes, it appears that his memo did not have the desired effect, as people continued to insist on using *contact* to mean "get in touch." It seems that he did, however, influence usage writers, especially E. B. White, who in the 1959 edition of Strunk and White's *Elements of Style* wrote that "As a transitive verb, the word is vague and self-important. Do not *contact* people; get in touch with them, look them up, phone them, find them, or meet them."[11]

The opinions of Messrs. Strunk, White, and Lienau notwithstanding, *contact* continued to flourish in common speech and writing throughout the twentieth century. The opinion of usage writers was divided as a number of them had already, by the 1960s, given up on attempting to restrict use of the word. A number of writers today continue to oppose this use of *contact*, although their ranks are greatly diminished.

I will cheerfully confess to using *contact* in this unapproved sense on occasion, without ever having given it much thought (which may be testament to either the increasing acceptance of the word or my own lack of standards). I will likely continue to so use it and will feel no guilt or shame about doing so. I will, however, attempt to use the word *cumber* more often, in honor of the splendid and splenetic memo writer from Western Union, Frederick W. Lienau.

four

Sins of Grammar

We often hear of the benefits of using correct grammar, and the perils of using it incorrectly. The former is viewed as indispensable to success, in one's professional and social endeavors. The latter is a stumbling block that will thwart one's ambitions, no matter how many other fine qualities one may possess.

Unfortunately, we have not yet been able to nail down exactly what good grammar is. To be sure, there are a number of things that most grammarians today agree are either right or wrong, but our language persists in changing, and the people who use it persist in ignoring the grammar rules that they find unwieldy or awkward; in many cases this will cause the rules to change over time to accommodate this usage. Complicating matters is the fact that the science of language study is a recent phenomenon: The application of modern linguistic tenets to English did not begin until the late nineteenth century. Many of the rules that we all think we should follow came from earlier grammarians, who were frequently armed with nothing more than a decent classical education and an abiding desire to correct the language of others.

Many grammarians of years gone by felt the need to build their reputations on the bodies of their slain colleagues and filled their books with attacks on the other writers who were trying to bring a sense of order to English. An example of this may be found in the debate over the issue of whether it was appropriate to use the phrase *grammatical error*.

Richard Meade Bache, writing in his 1868 book *Vulgarisms and Other Errors of Speech*, felt the need to open his chapter "Grammatical Errors" with a defense of the title: "The correctness of the expression 'grammatical errors' has been disputed. 'How,' it has been asked, 'can an error be grammatical?'"[1] According to some who thought long and hard about such matters, a grammatical error was a contradiction in terms (*grammatical* to them meant "having correct grammar" and so if it is an error it cannot be grammatical), and the preferred term should be *an error in grammar*.

This particular quibble has been put to rest, but we still have considerable disagreement in many areas as to what is correct grammar. As English spreads across the globe its variants become increasingly distinct from each other, yet for many there is a persistent belief that one true variant is grammatically correct.

The *Washington Post* published an article in 1908 that seemed to give evidence for some sort of irrefutable right and wrong of grammar: A professor had a dog who would whine when he heard improper grammar. "That 'Boojum,' the name of the animal, can distinguish between good and bad grammar is assuredly a fact," averred the paper.[2]

The dog did not only whine; apparently on one occasion he

became so distressed at a student's repeated use of *ain't* that he attacked the dialectical child and bit him on the leg. Boojum was obviously not actually learned in the finer points of syntax; he was but one in a long line of animals who were supposed to have human abilities in some field of knowledge. Boojum's predecessors include Clever Hans, a horse who was thought to be able to perform simple math and other intellectual feats, and Wicked Ben, a hog who was ostensibly very talented at playing euchre.

This chapter consists of entries on the abuse of word order, using an adjective when you should use an adverb, splitting infinitives, and doing other such things as make dogs bark.

SPLITTING INFINITIVES

> The practical arguments against the usage are three: (1) it is a vulgarism; (2) it always enfeebles the phrase; (3) it scarcely ever makes for cleverness.
> —William Archer, *Study and Stage: A Yearbook of Criticism* (addressing the subject of split infinitives), 1899

> [W]hen I split an infinitive, God damn it, I split it so it will remain split.
> —Raymond Chandler, in letter to Edward Meeks, 1947

You might be familiar with the voice-over from the beginning of the television show *Star Trek* (the original series), which contains the portentous phrase "To boldly go where no man has gone before." It is sometimes held up as an example of misuse by those who track the split infinitive and would like to kill it. It is also proudly held up as an example of how an infinitive can be happily split.

(For those of you who do not know what an infinitive is, don't feel bad. Should anyone tease you about this lack of knowledge, you might point out that people used to know what datives, genitives, accusatives, and imperatives were, and few people know what these are today. You can always say that you are following English in its inexorable march away from being a case-inflected language. That will quiet those who are bullying you.)

An infinitive verb is widely considered to be the construction *to* + (verb), as in *to criticize* or *to correct*. *Star Trek*, in the eyes and ears of some, spat upon the English language in contempt when the writers inserted that *boldly* between the *to* and the *go*. Most linguists, however, refuse to accept this definition of the split infinitive, as they feel, rightly, that the word *to* is not actually part of the infinitive. But assuming you are not talking to a linguist, when you hear someone talking about splitting an infinitive, they mean putting a word, commonly an adverb, between the *to* and the verb.

The writers of *Star Trek* were obviously not the first ones to split an infinitive, nor were they the first to boldly split the infinitive form of *to go* with the adverb *boldly*; nineteenth-century literature has many examples of writers using "to boldly go," and no one complained about the mistreatment of *boldly*. There was, however, complaint about the splitting of other verbs, even though, oddly enough, the complaints about splitting an infinitive began before we even had the phrase *split infinitive*. The infinitive was not referred to as being split until the end of the nineteenth century.*

----

* The earliest current evidence for this term is from 1890, in an article titled "A Novel in Journalese" in the *Scots Observer*: "the split infinitive ('to solemnly curse') is a captain jewel in the carcanet."

The proscription against splitting the infinitive did not originate, as did so many other rules, with the grammarians of the eighteenth century; it appears to have begun to annoy people in the following century. Bishop Lowth has long been accused of being the first to get his knickers in a twist over the split.

Lowth was responsible for popularizing a great number of other peeves about the English language, and his name has become, at least in some circles, synonymous with a sort of punctilious nitpickery (he was perhaps the only grammarian to have had a website devoted to him, which is now sadly defunct, titled "Bishop Lowth Was a Fool"). It is understandable that he should be blamed for introducing this rule, as he was also the man we hold responsible for formulating or popularizing many of the most cherished prescriptive beliefs, but in this instance he has been unfairly maligned. For nowhere in any of his writings do we find him displeased with the split infinitive, or even mentioning it.

Once someone finally sat down and read everything Lowth ever wrote, it was realized that he never said anything about the split infinitive; credit for prohibiting it was given to Richard Taylor, who certainly had written about the split infinitive and abhorred it, writing in 1840: "Some writers of the present day have a disagreeable affectation of putting an adverb between *to* and the infinitive."[3]

Next, intrepid sleuths found an article in the *New England Magazine*, written in 1834 by an anonymous correspondent, who expresses displeasure with the fact that kids these days were doing such horrible things to the language, especially the verbs. He opined that there was no rule protecting the defenseless infinitives from the predations of "uneducated persons" and offered himself as an arbiter on how one should treat verbs and adverbs, and the proper placement of each.[4] For a number of years this anonymous writer has been seen as the earliest complaint against the split infinitive.

As much as I would love to see that untold millions of hours of grammatical argument and finger-pointing had been caused by one faceless author writing a whinging complaint in a magazine in 1834, it is not quite the case.

In 1803, an obscure grammarian named John Comly published *English Grammar, Made Easy to the Teacher and Pupil*, which contained within it the following rule: "An adverb should not be placed between a verb of the infinitive mood and the preposition *to* which governs it; as "*Patiently* to wait"; "*Quietly* to hope."[5] It would be somewhat surprising if Comly indeed turns out to have been the first person to formulate this prohibition, but he provides, for now, the earliest evidence of any rule.*

The split infinitive has a name that fits its history rather well, as the use of the construction itself was split between two distinct periods of English. Split infinitives did not begin to be used until Middle English, for the simple reason that in Old English it was not possible to split them. Old English is a highly inflectional language, much as Latin is, and the infinitive form of the verb was a single word with a specific ending on it. There are not two words in the infinitive that you could place a word between, so it just wasn't done. Even though it is impossible to split the infinitive in both Latin and Old English, the reasons given by nineteenth-century grammarians who prescribed against splitting is because

---

* Considering his writing style, we should be grateful that Comly has not had more of an influence: His definition of a noun, somewhat more verbose than "person, place, or thing," was "the name of any thing that we can see, hear, taste, smell, feel, or discourse of."

it couldn't be done in Old English; they always reference the precedent of Latin. This was a common notion; that we should try to make English conform to the rules of what was widely viewed as a more *noble* language.

Infinitives were first split in the thirteenth century, as English continued its transformation from being a highly inflected language that is very difficult to learn to its present state of being a less inflected language that is very difficult to learn. They would pop up occasionally—Chaucer used them, as did Wycliffe. They never approached plague levels, except in the writings of one man, named Reginald Pecock, a fifteenth-century writer and the bishop of Chichester.

Pecock split his infinitives far more than any other writer before him[6] and more than any writer to follow for hundreds of years.* He split with a vengeance, placing not only single adverbs but large clauses amid his infinitives.† He met an unhappy end, being removed as bishop and having much of his published writing burned (although this was due to charges of religious, rather than grammatical, heresy).[7]

Then a peculiar thing happened: They split, these cut-up infinitives, in the sense meaning "they disappeared." The split infinitives existed in English for approximately four hundred years, and then seemingly all got together telepathically, decided they

---

* A professor in the early twentieth century reviewing Pecock's work referred to his habit of splitting his infinitives as "deplorably modern."

† "Sone, it is forto, at sum whilis, whanne oþire final seruycis of god, aftir doom of resound more profitable to be doon, schulen not þerbi to be lettid, and whanne a man in his semyng haþ rede to meke bisynes for to gendre freendful goostly loue toward god or toward him silf, worchipe and honoure god." The Middle English may give some of you a headache, but what is noteworthy is that he has almost fifty words between his *forto* and his *worchipe*.

didn't want to be used anymore, and left the language for a few hundred years. No one is entirely sure why they did this.

For almost the entirety of the sixteenth through eighteenth centuries you will be very hard-pressed to find any split infinitives, although there are exceptions. Shakespeare used it only once, in Sonnet 142: "Thy pity may deserve to pitied be." Samuel Butler likewise split his infinitive once in *Hudibras* in 1684, placing a *not* between his *to* and his *appear*, "And if we had not weighty Cause To not appear in making Laws, We could, in spight of all your Tricks, and Shallow, formal Politicks, Force you, our Managements t'obey."[8] Perhaps Butler and Shakespeare tried this usage, decided they did not care for the taste, and spat it out. In any event, the use of the split infinitive in these centuries is exceedingly rare.

This is something that I imagine must be exceedingly vexatious to grammar teachers who have spent countless hours trying to teach students not to split their infinitives: Somewhere in the long lost history of English there is a sort of holy grail that conveys the ability to make a usage problem disappear from the language almost entirely. And we don't know how it was accomplished. One thing we can be certain of is that it was not accomplished through the painstaking labor of English teachers, as no one at that point was complaining about the practice.

The split infinitive, like a linguistic cicada, lay dormant for hundreds of years, reappeared at the end of the eighteenth century, and then began to spread with remarkable rapidity. As the number of split infinitives multiplied, so too did its detractors.

The question of whether or not this kind of word order is entirely wrong has never been fully settled. As far back as the 1850s the split infinitive has had defenders. Goold Brown, writing in *The Grammar of English Grammars* in 1851,[9] allowed that poets should be able to use them, although he thought that it was more elegant to place the adverb before the *to*. Brown, however, was in the minority opinion for the next hundred years or so, as most authorities felt that the practice was much to be frowned upon. In the late nineteenth and early twentieth centuries it is not uncommon to see it referred to in somewhat hysterical language; it is an "abomination,"[10] "an ugly thing,"[11] and "a weed which grows rankly in the garden of the journalist."[12] Today, our culture is fairly accepting of split infinitives, with many people who watch over language reasoning that there is no reason why we should continue to force a Latinate structure on our Germanic language. Some grammar guides say that there is nothing wrong with splitting infinitives, while a diminishing number continue to insist that it is flat wrong. Still others attempt to hedge their bets, arguing that while it may not be wrong there are enough people who might be offended by seeing anything come between a *to* and its verb that it is advisable to not use them.

One of the more curious admonishments still given as to why split infinitives should be avoided is that they sound "inelegant." It is undoubtedly true that split infinitives can provide the linguistic equivalent of wearing a plaid tie with a striped shirt, but it is also true that *not* splitting an infinitive can sometimes sound inelegant as well.

Consider the sentence: "I decided to slowly begin to use more split infinitives in my writing," meaning that I will begin using more and more of them as time goes on. There is no way to unsplit that infinitive without changing the meaning of the sentence. If one writes "I decided slowly to begin . . . ," it sounds as if my decision itself comes slowly, and if the sentence reads "I decided to begin to use more infinitives in my writing slowly," it just sounds horrible.

Once we've established that sometimes it's inelegant to split the infinitive and sometimes it's inelegant not to split it, well, I think that we've arrived at the point where it must be admitted that the state of the infinitive isn't that important. What we are actually saying here is that bad writing is inelegant and good writing is not. So strive for the latter and leave the talk of infinitives out of it.

DIFFERENT THAN

> In any case, the phrase "different than" is almost never correct. Remember that "than" is used only with comparatives—words with "more" in front of them or with "-er" attached at the end. "Different than" can be correct only when it is *more* different than."
>
> —*MBA Center GMAT Study Book*, 2006

> This time the subject is a formal argument composed of premises and conclusions which is no different than the arguments you'll find in the Critical Reasoning section.
>
> —*MBA Center GMAT Study Book*, 2006

The imbroglio over what sort of preposition should follow the adjective *different* has been simmering since at least 1770, when Robert Baker weighed in against it in his *Remarks on the English Language*. This guide to English usage was curiously influential, insofar as it had any influence whatsoever. Baker proudly and inexplicably boasted of his ignorance and lack of education. In the preface to his book he stated that he has "paid no Regard to Authority," has "censured even our best Penman," and "not being acquainted with any Man of Letters, I have consulted Nobody"[13] as well as noting that he "quitted the School at fifteen."[14] None of these served as an obstacle to his passing judgment on how the language should best be used by others, even those who presumably had not "quitted the school."

Baker's consultation of nobody is occasionally evident in his writing, as he exhibits some curious discrepancies. At one point he boldly states that "*A different Manner than* is not English. We say *different to* and *different from.*" Shortly after giving his benediction to *different to* he writes "I would therefore give my Vote for *different from*, and would banish the Expression of *different to.*" There is no evidence that people were concerned by this issue before Baker, but the issue has since annoyed many careful users of language.

The dichotomous beginning found in Baker is fitting, as there has never been any widespread agreement between the way that *different* is prescribed and the way that it is used. *Different than* has been stomping through English since the middle of the seventeenth century, when it first rudely pushed *different to* and *from* out of the way and howled its unspeakable name.* *Different from* and *to* both have been used since the sixteenth century. The *OED* informs us that *different than* "is found in Fuller, Addison, Steele, De Foe, Richardson, Goldsmith, Miss Burney, Coleridge, Southey, De Quincey, Carlyle, Thackeray, Newman, Trench, and Dasent, among others." None of this has had much influence in changing the feelings of people such as novelist Meredith Nicholson, who

----

* It appears in Thomas Jordan's 1641 *Pictures of Passion, Fancies, and Affectations*: "although we may Conclude, nought is more different than they."

in 1922 wrote "Within a few years the abominable phrase different than has spread through the country like a pestilence."[15]

Following Baker's dictum the cudgel against placing anything but *from* after *different* was taken up by a number of other grammarians, and while there has never been a clear victory over the use of *than*, the campaign was successful in instilling in many people a vague sense of unease with their own natural way of speaking or writing, and *from* outweighs *than* in most corpora of published writing, although *than* retains a healthy minority.

Baker's desire to banish it from the language notwithstanding, *different to* likewise managed to survive and thrive in all levels of speech and writing, although it is almost entirely confined to British English.

The most common argument against the use of *different than* is that *than* should be used after a comparative adjective, and *different*, while certainly an adjective, is not a comparative one. This line of reasoning is disputed by some, on the grounds that *different* can indeed function as a comparative adjective.* It is disputed by others on the grounds that this is a ridiculous thing to get worked up about. Whether or not *different* is in fact a comparative, it is certain that people who use *different than* are using it in this way. In *The Plays of William Shakespeare*, Samuel Johnson wrote "Shakespeare confounds words more different than *proprietor* and *protector*," using *different* as a comparative.[16]

However, if one does believe that *different* is the adjectival

- - - - - - - - - - - - - - - - - -

* For those who are too embarrassed to admit that they do not know what a comparative adjective is (or too lazy to go look it up), it is an adjective that indicates a degree of comparison. Usually this is done through the addition of -*er* (as in *taller* or *shorter*), but occasionally there are exceptions (such as *worse*).

form of the verb "to differ," it would be clumsy, at best, to say that something *differs than*, whereas to say that it *differs from* is perfectly fine. I suppose that one could always try to make *different* into an obvious comparative, but something tells me that *differenter than* is unlikely to lower the hackles of people who prefer *different from*.

It is not terribly difficult to find cases where inflicting *different from* upon a sentence, rather than *different than*, would result in a hypercorrect monstrosity, or would create the need to rewrite much of the sentence. When Ernest Hemingway wrote "things in the night are different than they are in the day"[17] it sounds very much like something that he would write. "Things in the night are different from what they are in the day" doesn't quite work, and "things in the night are different from the way that they are in the day" sounds awkward, and very much like something that Hemingway would not have written.

Some usage guides have come to the conclusion that *different than* can be used, when it is preceded by the word *more* (although *different from* is still preferred when one has a choice). An example of this can be found in James Greenwood's *Essay Towards a Practical English Grammar*, which helpfully uses both forms in the same sentence: "it is more *different from* the Welch, than either the Cornish Language, or that of Bretagne in France, but scarcely more *different than* the modern German is from the English."[18] Had he written "but scarcely more *different from* the modern German," it would have created a muddle of the sentence. But fret not, for you needn't carry an additional supply of *mores* around in your pocket, in case you feel the need to use *different than*.

In the cases where *different than* is viewed as acceptable, the word *than* serves as a conjunction, joining a subordinate clause to a main one. In such cases it makes perfect grammatical sense to use *different than*. And it is important to note that this holds true even if the subordinate clause is elliptical, which I'll explain in a minute.

One of the problems with some modern usage guides is that they assume a level of proficiency on the part of their readers that is highly optimistic. Many of them will succinctly say that it is fine to use *different than* in cases in which it will be followed by a subordinate clause, whether elliptical or not, without providing any explanation as to what subordinate clauses do and how the elliptical examples of these creatures function. This is all well and good, except that the two categories of "people who are not sure what a subordinate clause is" and "people who consult English language usage guides" very often overlap with each other quite considerably. Now, if you are one of those people who is extremely proud that you know everything there is to know about subordinating clauses, elliptically or otherwise, pat yourself on the back and go back to being the person at the party no one wants to sit next to.

For the rest of you, a subordinate clause is a part of a sentence that conveys information but cannot stand on its own, and which contains a noun and a predicate (something that gives information about the noun). And saying that something is elliptical, in grammatical terms, means that there is a word, or words, that can be left out, while still conveying meaning. If you say "My feelings about you are different than before" this is an elliptical way of saying "My feelings about you are different than (they were) before."

There is really no way for me to make the description of elliptical subordinate clauses a sexy and engaging topic, so I will cease boring the reader and move on.

BUT/AND

It irks when nouns are used as verbs, apostrophes are left off (or misplaced), compound adjectives (such as UN-led) are not hyphenated, and sentences are begun with "But" or "However."
—Alan Duncan, Member of Parliament, in a memo sent to Britain's Department of International Development, 2012

But if there should remain two or more who have equal Votes, the Senate shall chuse from them by Ballot the Vice President.
—Article II, Section 1, Constitution of the United States, 1787

We all have linguistic shibboleths, standards of usage that we hold dear and use to make ourselves feel better about our language (and worse about the language of others). And while the word *shibboleth* itself has now taken on a variety of meanings, it is rooted in one of the darker chapters of the history of judging people based on how they use language.

In the Book of Judges, in the Old Testament of the Bible, there is a story of how Jephthah, commander of an army of Israelites, used the ancient Hebrew word *shibboleth* as a test with which to distinguish his own men from his vanquished enemies, the Ephraimites, who apparently had the bad habit of leaving out the initial *H* sound, pronouncing it *sibboleth*. Following a battle with the Ephraimites, Jephthah lined everyone up and had them say the word; those who pronounced it incorrectly, at least according to his standards, were summarily executed. The practice of using uniforms to distinguish between armies was apparently not yet in vogue.

Jephthah appears to have had several other questionable characteristics, not least among them the reputed sacrifice of his own daughter (some sources have it that he offered merely her eternal virginity as a sacrifice, rather than her life) as well as the fact that he was the sworn enemy of a fellow named Ammon. But we should not hold these peccadillos against him (not the Ammon-enmity, certainly), at least not in a book on language.

Among the shibboleths on language, few are more entrenched than the one about beginning a sentence with *and* or *but*. It is one of the capricious rules of language that we parrot, something that we all "know" is wrong without paying much attention to why this is the case. It also provides a fine illustration of how some myths about language tend to linger in the face of insurmountable evidence indicating that they should not.

The use of *and* to begin a sentence dates back at least to the year 855, as it is found in *The Old English Chronicle* about that time. Writers have been obliviously and happily breaking this not-yet written rule and beginning their sentences with it ever since. Our literature, at every level, is rife with sentences beginning with *and* or *but*. They appear in everything from Chaucer's "The Portrait of the Parson"* to Strunk and White's *Elements of Style*.†

Style guides of every stripe agree that there is nothing at all wrong with beginning a sentence with *and* or *but*. Fowler's *Dictionary of Modern English Usage* refers to it as "a faintly lingering superstition." Bryan Garner, in his *Modern American Usage*, is slightly more heated and calls it "rank superstition." *Merriam-Webster's*

----

* "But riche he was of hooly thought and werke."

† "But do not assume that because you have acted naturally your product is without flaw."

Dictionary of English Usage states that "Everybody agrees that it's all right to begin a sentence with and, and nearly everybody admits to having been taught at some past time that the practice was wrong."

So even though this rule was found to be at best questionable, well over a hundred years ago, we still find people who cling to it. A letter to the editor, published in the *Providence Journal* on July 11, 2004, made this case in a rather martial fashion. One George Quinn, the letter writer in question, began his missive by stating that "After reading Bob Kerr's June 23 column, it was embarrassingly obvious that he was never beaten in school. Had he been appropriately beaten in grammar class, he might have learned the role of the conjunction." Quinn goes on to point out that the offending columnist "began eight sentences with either 'and' or 'but.' Those words belong to the part of speech that connects; they don't begin a sentence."

Putting aside for a moment whether we should or should not be taking advice on any use of language from a man who employs the phrase "appropriately beaten in grammar class," it is worth noting that his sentiments are not unusual. Where did this notion come from, and why has it proved, in the face of such overwhelming disputation, to be so intractable?

The logic behind not beginning sentences with *and* or *but* is based on the fact that they are coordinating conjunctions, and so should be found bridging two parts within a sentence. The first glimmers of prescribing against placing a conjunction at the front of a sentence come at the very end of the eighteenth century, appearing more as a peevish whine than a set rule. In William Burdon's *Examination of the Merits and Tendency of the Pursuits of Literature,* he comments unfavorably of another writer: "I must

frequently have occasion to object to the Author's mode of punctuation; he for ever begins a sentence with a conjunction or an
adverb,—an *if,* or an *and.*"[19]

There were few, if any, grammarians writing about this in the
beginning of the nineteenth century. Perhaps the first to make a
specific pronouncement on it was George Payn Quackenbos, a
noted educator and writer on language and history. In addition
to writing books as widely ranging as *Phraseology of Roman Sepul-
chral Inscriptions* and *A Primary History of the United States, Made Easy
and Interesting for Beginners,* Quackenbos wrote *An Advanced Course
of Composition and Rhetoric,* the first edition of which appeared in
1854. In his chapter "The Period," he wrote "A sentence should
not commence with the conjunctions and, for, or however; but
may do so with but, none, and moreover."[20]

In 1868, George Washington Moon made mention of the subject in his scathing denunciation of another grammarian, titled
(just in case anyone missed the point) *The Bad English of Lindley
Murray and Other Writers on the English Language.** According to
Moon, "It is not scholarly to begin a sentence with the conjunction
and."[21] He makes no mention of whether it is also unscholarly or
boorish to begin a sentence with the conjunction *but,* but we can
safely assume that he does not have similar feelings for this conjunction, as he used it to begin his very next sentence.[22]

Before this, most people writing and speaking English felt no
compunction about beginning their sentences with *and* or *but,* or
even the occasional *however.* Various translations of the Bible are

----

* This was not Moon's only foray into the field of fixing other grammarians' writings.
He also wrote a book titled *The Dean's English,* which was entirely devoted to correcting what he perceived to be the errors of Henry Alford, the dean of Canterbury and
author of *A Plea for the Queen's English.*

chock-full of sentence-initial *and*'s ("And God said, Let there be light: and there was light") and *but*'s ("But Noah found grace in the eyes of the Lord"). In fact, in the eighteenth century, it was not uncommon to see and held up as a fine way to begin a sentence. James Greenwood, in *The Royal English Grammar* (1744) said of *and* that "it is a copulative, and joins sentences together."[23]

A number of grammarians subsequent to Greenwood disagreed with him on this score, reasoning that *and* and similar conjunctions should conjunct themselves only in the middle of a sentence and not at the beginning. But by and large, the feeling among writers of usage guides was that there was nothing wrong with so beginning a sentence. Using *however* to begin a sentence was still prescribed against by some (William Strunk's 1918 *Elements of Style* said of this word that "In the meaning nevertheless, not to come first in its sentence or clause."[24]) Despite the benediction given by some usage guides, there persisted in certain quarters the notion that certain words just weren't appropriate to use when beginning a sentence.

A pamphlet titled "Documents of the School Committee of the City of Boston," published in 1916 stressed that educators should "Teach the elimination of 'but,' 'so,' 'and,' 'because,' at the beginning of a sentence."[25] A book published in 1922, *Art and Science of Selling*, held that "It is not considered the best form however, to begin a sentence with a word ending in 'ing.'"[26] Jacob Cloyd Tressler continued the war against sentence-initial *however* and its sickly brethren with his 1929 book, *English in Action*, stating, "Do not begin a sentence with however or a similar unimportant word."[27]

Tressler did not see fit to explain exactly why *however* was unimportant or what other words might merit this distinction, but there are a fair number of words that have at one time or another been told they cannot stand at the front of the line. In addition to those already mentioned, there have been proscriptions about using numerous other words, including *nevertheless, for, nor, or, yet, also*, and *whether*. Some people will have a nagging and unpleasant memory of being handed some sheet of paper at the start of a past English class with the acronym FANBOYS written on it (*for, and, nor, but, or, yet, so*) designating what words one should not use to begin a sentence.

The prohibition against using words such as *and* to begin a sentence has some reasonable aspects to it. One such concern is that the words *and* and *but* sound as though they are going to introduce a dependent clause, rather than a full sentence, and thus are jarring to the ear of the listener. Additionally, there are some poor unfortunates who committed such egregious language sins in a past life that they were reincarnated as high school composition teachers, and they have been heard to make the case for banning *and* at the beginning of a sentence on the grounds that their students would otherwise use them too much. No one wants to read a book report that contains seventeen consecutive sentences beginning with *and* or any other word. If this is the case, these teachers have my sympathies, but there is still no reason to try to retain an entirely illogical rule in an attempt to avoid this. As in many other cases, the desired results can be better effected by teaching students how to write better.

It would be far more effective to try to ban the beginning of sentences with *and* or *but* on the grounds that they sound like they will introduce dependent clauses, rather than to simply say that they always have been and always will be coordinating conjunctions, but most people who hold on to this rule are simply parroting a rule that they learned long ago, one without such subtle explanation. Any attempt to curtail the overuse of some common practice by stating that it is always wrong is unlikely to meet with much success. To tell students that it is improper to do something that they then see everyone else doing quite naturally serves only to convince them that the grammar rules they are taught are arbitrary.

If you should have someone tell you that you have committed an error in beginning a sentence with *and*, and do not care to point to the Bible as your precedent, you can always quote the authority Robert Burchfield, a man who served as the editor for the *Oxford English Dictionary*. Burchfield said that "an initial and is a useful aid to writers as the narrative continues."[28] Considering the tiresome and prolonged nature of this narrative, we're going to need these *and*'s.

FUN

> Fun is not an adjective; it is a noun. While you can have fun, you cannot have a "fun time." A party can be fun but it does not then become a "fun" party. Please, no more "fun" movies.
> —Richard Block, *The Santa Fe New Mexican*, February 2, 2002

> It was fun to peer over one's third drink at the painted little people skimming along, losing a ski here, a pole there, or victoriously veering in a spray of silver powder.
> —Vladimir Nabokov, *Transparent Things*, 1972

For those of you who missed having your palms whacked with a ruler in English class on the day that the prohibition against the phrase "so fun" was handed out, here is the quick and dirty explanation for why you should apparently not do so: *fun* is not an adjective. It is a noun, and if you try to use it adjectivally you might as well say "that was so enjoyment."

Now, you may have been using this word in an adjectival manner, as have millions of other wayward souls who were born after the middle of the twentieth century, but you also are probably the kind of person who refers to the cloth things that hang over your windows as *drapes*,* so your judgment is obviously not to be trusted. Because, according to numerous sources of correct usage, this word that you have been using to signify enjoyment does not actually exist.

Fun entered English in the seventeenth century and originally referred to something that was not very much fun at all: It was both a noun (meaning "a hoax") and a verb ("to cheat"). The *Oxford English Dictionary* records the first instance of the word as a noun occurring in the *New Dictionary of the Canting Crew*, which was a sort of guide to the slang of the criminal class, put together so that honest people might know the language of thieves and mendicants and not be swindled by them. *Fun* began its life as a verb and noun more or less simultaneously.

Shortly thereafter the noun form of *fun* began to be used in the sense of "something diverting or amusing," although it was still thought to be, in Samuel Johnson's words "a low cant word."[29] It was not until the middle of the nineteenth century that *fun* began to be used as an adjective, in the sense that we frequently use it today.

There is speculation that *fun* sneaked into its new part of

---

* The etiquette expert Emily Post, writing in 1933, said that "'Drapes' is utterly vulgar—in fact, no word is a greater offense to good taste, not even 'gents.'"

speech as an attributive noun. These sneaky bastards are nouns that function as adjectives, as in *college student*. The word *college* is certainly a noun, but in this case it modifies the next noun, *student*, and so we would refer to it as an attributive noun. *Fun* began to be used in this sense in the middle of the nineteenth century (the *OED* records the first such use as "fun room," from 1846).

Once *fun* had established a beachhead on our language as an attributive noun it executed the next step in its dastardly plan and began functioning as an outright adjective (in such uses as "the party was fun"). This is a reasonable route for a word to take, yet the adjectival use of *fun* has continued to irritate many people, as can be seen in the resistance that so many people feel when confronted with the words *funner* or *funnest*. If we accept that *fun* is in fact an adjective as well as a noun and a verb, there is no logical reason why we shouldn't modify it the same way we would modify similar adjectives.

You can use *funner* and *funnest*, but you should bear in mind that anyone who chastises you for this use is unlikely to be interested in hearing your explanation for why it should be acceptable. These words will grate on the ears of many for some while to come. The process of an acceptable usage becoming unacceptable can be a long one, and the reverse process is true as well. Just because you *can* do something does not mean that you *should*.

But no matter whether you accept *funnest* or not, it is clear that *fun* has taken on full citizenship as an adjective. The word has transformed itself from thieves' slang to common usage, picking up new parts of speech and shedding others. It mirrors the prototypical American success story of reinvention. As such a successfully reinvented word, *fun* deserves some measure of recognition, of the kind given by Dwight Bolinger, who referred to it as "a shining example of the gradual emancipation of a form once securely barricaded behind the wall that separates nouns from adjectives."[30]

THAT/WHICH

That is often used, but inelegantly, for *who*, *whom*, and *which*.
—James Buchanan, *A Regular English Syntax*, 1769

The tendency among mediocre writers of American English is to use *which* instead of *that* when it follows a plural noun, and the other way around when it follows a singular noun.
—Adam Garfinkle, *Political Writing: A Guide to the Essentials*, 2012

The rules governing when one should use *which* or *who* and when one should use *that* are beloved by copy editors, and members of this tribe will defend these rules to the last. Most other people have long since given up on this matter or didn't know that there was much difference in the first place. However, should you ever wish to meet and woo a copy editor or be faced with the prospect of having one of these fearsome creatures as an in-law, you might want to know the difference between them.

To the copy editor, there is little room here for debate: One either knows where to put one's thats and whiches or one does not. Unfortunately for the rest of us, the history and practice of this matter are somewhat confusing.

Grammar guides today abound with forceful rules for how one should employ these words. However, breaking down whether you should use *that*, *which*, or *who* requires an explanation of restrictive and nonrestrictive relative clauses, the mere mention of which, I am afraid, has the ability to render most readers immediately glassy-eyed. To make this as short and brutal an explanation as possible, think of a restrictive clause as a liver: a vital organ of the sentence that cannot be removed without killing it. A nonrestrictive clause, however, is more like the appendix or tonsils of a sentence: It may be desirable to have but can be removed without dying (so long as one does so carefully).

Restrictive clauses give the reader essential information about the noun or phrase that precedes them. "That was the grammar class that I hated so much" is a sentence that contains a restrictive relative clause. If you remove this clause ("that I hated so much") your sentence will die. If, however, you look at a sentence such as "The grammar class, which I very much hated, was in this building," you will see that it has a nonrestrictive relative clause ("which I very much hated") that can be removed without killing the sentence. One explanation that is often offered is that if you need to use a comma you should be using which instead of that.

"Why is this important?" some might ask. After all, most of you have managed to successfully navigate the shoals of life so far without having to waste valuable synaptic connections on identifying nonrestrictive relative clauses, and you would be excused for wondering why this horrid writer is trying to explain some concept that will push out important information stored in your brain, such as the color of your child's eyes or the memory of the first time you noticed that your husband was repeating the stories he told you.

The reason this information is important is that it provides the basis for how modern grammarians have decided which relative pronoun should be used. The word *modern* is necessary here since the current rules on this issue are not very old.

In the mid-eighteenth century there were rules governing the use of *who, that,* and *which,* but they were not quite the same as the ones we have today. In fact, they were decidedly different. The first mention of what one should do with the word *that* came in *Observations Upon the English Language*, when George Harris wrote that "the word THAT ought never to be used as an article relative." He felt that writers should instead only use *who* for referring to people and *which* in referring to things.[31]

The *Merriam-Webster Dictionary of English Usage* points out that *that* had a long and distinguished career in English as a relative pronoun and for several hundred years writers blithely swapped *that* and *which* without worrying about it. That fell into disuse (in writing, at least) in the latter half of the seventeenth century, before coming back into favor later in the eighteenth.[32]

Henry Alford's mid-nineteenth-century book *A Plea for the Queen's English* offers a view of the resurgent *that*: after noting that *who* is used to refer to people and *which* is used for things, he writes "now we do not commonly use either the one or the other of these pronouns, but make the more convenient one, 'that' do duty for both."[33] Another grammar guide published at that time, *Wells's School Grammar*, likewise explains that "who is applied to persons," while *which* is used for "irrational animals and things without life." Although Wells also says that *that* can be used in place of either *who* or *that*, he offers no restrictions on how it should so be done.[34]

Thus by the end of the nineteenth century we had a fairly clear and simple set of rules for how to use these three relative pronouns: *who* referred to people, *which* was used for things and irrational animals, and *that* could be used to refer to either. If it was all so simple why do so few people today feel like they have a handle on this? Enter the Fowlers.

The brothers Fowler (Francis George and Henry Watson) are often credited with formulating the modern rules behind the use of *which*, *that*, and *who*, in their 1906 book *The King's English*. Although the Fowlers were not the first to examine the issue of restrictive and nonrestrictive clauses (which they referred to as defining and nondefining), they are likely the first to have codified a set of rules for when to use *who*, *that*, and *which* within these clauses.

The first rule issued by the Fowlers is "'That' should never be used to introduce a non-defining clause."[35] They then proceed to offer a number of illustrative quotations from authors who have botched this over the years, including Thomas De Quincey, William Makepeace Thackeray, and George Meredith. These writers failed to adhere to this rule for the simple reason that it did not exist at the time that they were writing.

The second rule offered is "'Who' or 'which' should not be used in defining clauses except when custom, euphony, or convenience is decidedly against the use of 'that.'" There follows an enumeration of what some of these customs, euphonies, or conveniences might be, including not putting two *that*s in a row, alternating between *that* and *which* if there are two relative clauses in the same sentence, and allowing the use of the prepositional phrase *of which* in a defining clause. The Fowlers may have created a solution in search of a problem (I am aware that copy editors will vehemently disagree with this statement), but they at least did so with nuance and a degree of pragmatism. At the very beginning of their discussion of *that* vs. *which* they note that "it is not easy to draw any distinction that is at all consistently supported by usage." And after giving their list of exceptions they offer the caveat, "It may seem to the reader that a rule with so many exceptions to it is not worth observing." Henry Fowler even admitted that the rules he and his brother proposed were essentially failures. Twenty years after the publication of *The King's English*, he wrote of distinguishing between *that* and *which*, "it would be idle to pretend that it is the practice either of most or of the best writers."[36]

Although such nuance is a pleasing quality to have in a usage guide, it appears to have led to trouble for many Americans. Hordes of us have simply thrown our hands up in despair when faced with deciding whether our clauses were restrictive or not, and if we should use one of the many exceptions that the Fowlers offered. The British, on the other hand, took a more practical approach and decided they could use either *that* or *which* in their restrictive clauses (although they still insist on using *which* for nonrestrictive ones). The 2005 edition of *New Hart's Rules*, a style guide based on the rules for readers and compositors at Oxford University Press, states unequivocally "in restrictive relative clauses either which or that may be used."[37]

You should be warned that if you stick a *that* in a nonrestrictive relative clause (as in "This chapter, that is the more boring thing I have ever read, is about clauses") it runs a good chance of appearing awkward. However, most English speakers fluidly use *which* in both restrictive and nonrestrictive clauses and have been doing so for hundreds of years. We also have the tendency to substitute *that* for *who* in restrictive clauses ("There were three of us that failed the test"), although this will raise the hackles of some: David Foster Wallace referred to it as "the grammatical equivalent of wearing NASCAR paraphernalia or liking pro wrestling."[38]

If you have given up on impressing the copy editor in your life and would simply like some commonsensical advice that is not weighted with rules, you may follow the guidance of Porter Perrin and Wilma Ebbitt, who addressed this issue in their *Writer's Guide and Index to English*: "The choice between which and that in restrictive clauses is more likely to depend on rhythm, sound, emphasis, personal taste, and a desire to avoid repetition than on any rule."[39]

ENDING A SENTENCE WITH A PREPOSITION

> TEXAN: "Where are you from?"
> HARVARD STUDENT: "I am from a place where we do not end
>   our sentences with prepositions."
> TEXAN: "OK, where are you from, jackass?"
> —Variation on an old joke

Even the most fervent believers in the notion that one should never end a sentence with a preposition would be hard-pressed to live up to the example of the great seventeenth-century poet John Dryden, who so believed in this that he went and republished his *Essay of Dramatic Poesy*, sixteen years after it had first appeared, just so he could remove the prepositions from the end of the sentences.*

Dryden may have hated sentences that end with *of*, but it was something of a privately held peeve: He mentions his discomfort with the errant prepositions only twice in his writing. The first time was in 1672, when passing judgment upon the poetry of Ben Jonson: "The preposition in the end of the sentence; a common fault with him, and which I have but lately observed in my own writings."[40] He mentioned it for the second, and final, time in 1691, in response to a letter from a young poet: "I remember I

---

* Dryden also took this opportunity to clean up what he perceived to be other stylistic flaws in his writing, such as use of colloquialisms and multiword verbs.

hinted somewhat of concludding (*sic*) your sentences with prepositions or conjunctions sometimes, which is not elegant."[41]

No one is entirely certain where this bee in Dryden's bonnet came from. Some speculate that it may have been a desire to make his English conform more with Latin syntax, in which case there would be no way to end a sentence with a distinct preposition. Others speculate that he, like many other English writers of the seventeenth century, was influenced by French classical literature. And still others think that he was influenced by John Tillotson, the Archbishop of Canterbury and a widely admired writer of English prose.

All these theories are possible, some more so than others, but there is no overwhelming evidence in favor of any of them. Also possible is that Dryden simply decided that he didn't much care for prepositions at the end of sentences or that he was scolded as a child by a long-forgotten teacher for putting them there and so decided that he would institute this rule in his own writing.

There has been a widespread belief (among people who study such things) that Dryden invented this rule and that subsequent grammarians picked it up and enshrined it in the canon of "grammatical rules that are widely ignored." It would be pleasing if this were true: One of the most objectionable and illogical rules of English usage has as its origin nothing more logical than the spleen of a long-dead poet who once decided that he didn't like some part of the language and so set out to change it. However, it appears that Dryden had a predecessor in this, and this has been caught by a gimlet-eyed linguist.

Nuria Yáñez-Bouza is a professor of linguistics, specializing in the history of English presciptivism, with a subspecialty in attitudes toward sentences that end with a preposition (or, as the linguists would phrase it, preposition stranding). She is also a splendid example of how maniacally thorough academics can be with a subject when they find one that speaks to them, as she has written at least two theses, one full book (not to mention chapters on the subject in an additional four books), and several papers on the history of why so many of us have a vague feeling of unease when we see one of our sentences end with *of* or *with*.

Yáñez-Bouza found admonishments against the use of preposition stranding in the work of Joshua Poole, a not terribly well-known grammarian of the mid-seventeenth century. In a 1646 book titled *The English Accidence* Poole wrote of the importance of placing "the words in their naturall order." He advocated changing "whom did you give your book to?" to "to whom did you give your book?" and "this is the man I told you of" to "of whom I told you."

Poole's feelings on where the preposition should or should not go were motivated by a desire to have English conform more to the structure of Latin, a language in which one cannot strand a preposition at the end of a sentence. The fact that ending sentences with prepositions is common in Germanic languages (such as English) bothered him not at all. The idea that the rules of Latin should be applied to the English language by writers of this time is not surprising when one considers that English grammars were still occasionally being written in Latin (the last such curiosity was published in 1685).

Even though Dryden was not the first to call for cutting off terminal prepositions, it is likely that he should receive much of the credit for inflicting this rule upon subsequent generations, as he was certainly more widely read and emulated than Poole. But even if we credit Dryden for introducing this rule, it took a considerable length of time for it to take root.

Shortly after Dryden sanitized his *Essay of Dramatic Poesy* the English language entered the eighteenth century, a time when grammarians ruled the earth (or at least when they published a great many books). The second half of that century saw a plague of grammar books and usage guides, the likes of which the world had never seen before. Very few of the hundreds of such works were concerned with celebrating the beauty of the language; they were mainly alarmist rants about the way that English was being misused. Some of these grammarians echoed Dryden and Poole's discomfort with the end placement of prepositions. But for the most part, they didn't pay it much mind.

Bishop Lowth, in his *Short Introduction to English Grammar*, grudgingly admitted that joining a preposition to the verb at the end of a sentence was "an Idiom which our language is strongly inclined to"* but thought that it was "more graceful, as well as more perspicuous"[42] to move it forward in the sentence. The other eighteenth-century language guardians generally did not see the terminal preposition as threatening the sanctity of English. Some were actually in favor of placing it at the end of a sentence, such as Archibald Lane who, in his 1705 *A Key to the Art of Letters*, thought the phrasing "this is the person I spoke of" was elegant.[43]

By the end of the eighteenth century, however, grammarians got their ducks in a row and began to properly lay into the preposition at the end of the sentence. Hugh Blair, in his 1783 *Lectures*

----

* Which many people have pointed out could have been rephrased "to which our language is strongly inclined," as the preposition was thought to be improper at the end of clauses as well as of sentences.

on Rhetoric and Belles Lettres, wrote of sentences that one should "avoid concluding them with an adverb, a preposition or any inconsiderable word. Such sentences are always enfeebling and degrading."[44] *Enfeebling* and *degrading* are strong words, and they primed the writers who followed.

Noah Webster thought that this practice was allowable in conversation, but "in the grave and sublime styles, it is certainly inadmissible."[45] Brandon Turner, in *A New English Grammar,* wrote "It is, in general, ungraceful to end a sentence with an adverb, a preposition, or any inconsiderable word or phrase, which may either be earlier introduced or altogether omitted."[46]

For many of these writers the reason to avoid terminal prepositions was not simply that it violated proper syntax but that it was a weak way in which to end a sentence.[47] Presumably sentences should end with a bang, rather than a whimper. These sentences were not only "enfeebling and degrading," they were "inelegant,"[48] "a violation of grace,"[49] and provided a "want of dignity."[50] It is a fine thing to say that sentences should not end with a weak word, but expressing that by saying terminal prepositions should be avoided is simply muddying the issue.

This edict took a long time to be fully embraced by the grammarians, and it proved to have a short life. By the beginning of the twentieth century usage guides weren't just acquiescent to the notion that sentences could end with a preposition; they were scoffing at the notion that this practice should be avoided. But their acknowledgment that there's nothing wrong with the fact that we all end our sentences with prepositions has been ignored by many, and the rule continues to be bandied about today as one of those things that ostensibly proper writers observe.

For much of the past hundred years this bastard child of

Joshua Poole has been viewed as a rule. It is a rule that one can break, but still very much a rule that needs to be accounted for. In seeking to poke fun at people who still follow this rule, we tell jokes such as the one at the beginning of this entry. Or we reference Winston Churchill, who was famously reported to have written "This is the kind of tedious/arrant nonsense up with which I will not put," in response to an overweening staffer having removed a preposition from some of his writing. (However, as with many quotes that are purported to have originated with the former prime minister of Great Britain, the author was someone other than Churchill).*

There are few, if any, guides to the English language today that give any credence to the notion that one should not end a sentence with a preposition. The no-terminal-prepositions restriction brought a knife to the gunfight with common usage, and it now lies supine and bloodied on the floor. The *American Heritage Dictionary*, generally regarded as having a prescriptive bent, says "English syntax not only allows but sometimes even requires final placement of the preposition."[51] Bryan Garner, in *Modern American Usage*, calls the rule "spurious,"[52] and even Strunk and White say "Not only is the preposition acceptable at the end, sometimes it is more effective in that spot than anywhere else."[53] The idea that it is wrong to end a sentence with a preposition has been opposed by almost all grammarians for almost a century, to say nothing of linguists, who have been against it for even longer.

However, there are still two places where one may find calls

----

* This particular example has been disproved by Ben Zimmer, language columnist for the *Wall Street Journal*, in an article written for the blog *Language Log* (itre.cis. upenn.edu/~myl/languagelog/archives/001715.html).

for adherence to this rule. The first is in Internet comments. This is unsurprising, as these frequently serve as bastions for the ill-informed and bilious of many stripes. The second holdout is a bit more puzzling: college writing centers.

The writing center at the University of Nevada, Las Vegas, warns "In formal writing, avoid ending a sentence with a preposition when you can do so without the resulting sentence structure being a tortured one."[54] Arizona State University has a Web page that hews to this line as well, telling students "Generally, you should try not to end your sentences with prepositions; this is especially true for formal, academic writing."[55] A Web page from the University of Iowa, titled "Common Errors to Avoid on Term Papers," states: "It has become acceptable to end a sentence with a preposition in conversational speech. Term papers, however, should not be written in conversational language."[56] No, presumably they should be written in the language of eighteenth-century linguistic scolds.

That the rule should continue to exist in the lower intestine of some websites is of little concern; the impotent rants of anonymous Internet commenters should have a negligible effect. But it is quite distressing to see it being actively taught in colleges and universities. The fact that these schools are still teaching this is similar to if they had decided to bring back the long *S*, capitalize all substantive nouns, and use *thou* for the second person singular, rather than *you*. Our greatest hope in overcoming this nonsense lies in the fact that the college students to whom these warnings are addressed will likely pay them no more mind than anything else they are taught. Shortly after graduating they may have some notion that there is something that one shouldn't do to a preposition, but will be unable to recall quite what it is.

VERY

"I am very pleased to see you," is another error of speech. One should either say, "I am pleased" or "I am very much pleased."
—Josephine Turck Baker, *Correct English*, 1899

We shall be very pleased to see you in January, wherever we are.
—D. H. Lawrence, letter to Max Mohr, October 31, 1927.

By this point it is likely that you have already formed an opinion of whether or not you care for this book. Some of you might mention it to a friend or acquaintance and say "I am very interested in this book," while others might well say "I am very repulsed by this book." Whatever differences in opinion you have on the subject, you will at least have one area of commonality, which is that many grammar writers of yore would consider both of those statements to be incorrect.

To those who have not spent much time reading grammar guides of old it will be rather puzzling to hear that the phrase "I am very pleased to meet you" is not up to snuff. What in the world is wrong with saying you are pleased to meet someone? Aha! You have improperly used the adjectival *very* (as an intensifier) to modify *pleased*, which is the past participle of the verb *to please*. The reasoning here is that there should be an adverb, standing in as a buffer to shield *pleased* from *very*. In other words, you left out your *much*.

The cudgel against this use of *very* was first taken up in the middle of the nineteenth century, after the great philologist Friedrich Max Müller made mention of what he thought of as an Americanism: the habit we backwoods rubes had of saying we were "very pleased" or "very delighted." Müller was of the opinion that *very* was used only with adjectives and *much* was used to precede participles, although he noted that "It is by no means impossible, however, that this distinction . . . should disappear in time."

A number of American grammarians were quite upset with Müller's pronouncement. No, they did not say anything like "Come on, Müller! Everybody says 'very pleased' and you know it," although such *very* turns of phrase were not at all uncommon in the eighteenth and nineteenth centuries. The grammarians were upset that Müller labeled this use as an Americanism and pointed out, quite rightly, that the British had been using it for hundreds of years as well.

Once this use of *very* had been put into the category of "problem usage" people began trying to figure out just how much of a problem it was and what to do about it. It's never been an easy thing to decide on since the root of the problem lies in deciding what kind of participle you are dealing with. If it has become a full adjective, then it would be considered acceptable to simply slap a *very* in front of it. But if the participle retains some of its verb-ness, as *pleased* was thought to have done, then the proper way to phrase it would be "very much pleased."

In the first edition of *Modern English Usage*, Henry Fowler spent a considerable amount of space trying to tease out when it would be permissible to use *very* before a participle without using *much*. I must confess that many of the distinctions he makes are lost on me, and I suspect that they would likewise be lost on most people today, even among those who think of themselves as being exceptionally careful with their language.

For instance, Fowler writes that *tired* and *celebrated* are fine to modify with *very* on its own, on the grounds that these words have become "true" adjectives. However, *pleased* and *inconvenienced* still require a *much* in front of them, as they have not yet completed their journey to full adjectivehood.

If such subtlety of distinction is not beyond your ken I congratulate you, and hope that you have a long and fruitful life. Bear in mind that much of this life will be spent inwardly wincing at the absent *muches* you note in the speech of those who do not pay such attention to their language.

Very ran into trouble later in the twentieth century, when it began appearing on many lists of "words that shouldn't be used so much," on the grounds that poor writers use it to excess. Since questions of taste are outside of the purview of this book, I will not bore you with a long explanation of who has had what feelings regarding *very*, save to say that there is widespread feeling among many people that it is a largely unnecessary word.

In case this has left you feeling very (much) worried about whether you have been excluding the word *much* overmuch from your language, *very* is not the only word to receive such attention. *Too* (generally when used with *not*, as in "I was not too pleased to see him") has similarly been thought to be improper when placed directly in front of a past participle. However, the proscription against such use has come only from American grammarians, so should anyone accuse you of such a sin you can also pretend that you are British.

But even if you are profligate with your use of *very* and *too* and never met a *much* you cared to put after them, worry not. This rule is observed less and less frequently. A sign of this may be found in *Communication Skills in English*, a textbook published in India and designed for students who learn English as a second language. The authors offer the improperly worded sentence "I am too pleased to see you," and follow it with the correct version: "I am very pleased to see you."[57]

I VS. ME

> "It is me." Now this is an expression which every one uses. Grammarians (of the smaller order) protest: schoolmasters (of the lower kind) prohibit and chastise; but English men, women, and children go on saying it, and will go on saying it as long as the English language is spoken.
>
> —Henry Alford, *A Plea for the Queen's English*, 1864

> You sneer at "Americanisms," but you would never find an educated American who would venture to say "It is me" for "It is I"; or "It is him" for "It is he."
>
> —George Washington Moon, *The Dean's English*, 1864

There is an old *New Yorker* cartoon that nicely captures some of the confusion over whether one should use "it is I" or "it is me." The illustration shows an aggrieved-looking woman speaking to an unknown person on the other side of her heavily locked door, with the caption reading: "I don't know anybody who says 'It is I.'"

This is not the only instance in which the ostensibly correct use of *I* serves as a punch line. An old joke—one with numerous variations—has St. Peter asking the name of a supplicant at the gates of heaven. Upon hearing him proclaim "It is I," he responds "Go away, we have enough English teachers already." One would think, based on these examples, that the matter is settled.

But what is peculiar about this issue is the fact that the traditionally incorrect form (*me*) is still held up as something that one should not do, while at the same time the correct form (*I*) is frequently made fun of. It appears that the only safe response to the question, Who's there? is to give your name.

What's wrong about saying "It is me"? The easiest way to explain it is that when a pronoun (such as *I* or *me*) follows any form of the verb *to be* (such as *is*) it should be in the nominative case.

The nominative pronouns (for those of you who have forgotten such things and do not care to take out your phone to look it up) are *I, you, we, he, she, it*, and *they*. These are used to refer to the person who is the subject of the sentence. The objective pronouns are *me, you, us, him, her, it*, and *them*, and they are used to refer to the object of the sentence.

In the minds of the people who consider this an unpardonable lapse, the phrase *it is me* makes no more sense than were one to say "Him is my friend" or "Us consider poor grammar a sin." Such constructions do indeed sound odd, or at least highly questionable, yet countless numbers of us have happily adopted the similar "It is me." Why is this?

There has been a good amount written about how the phrase *it is me* came into the language. Theodore Visser, in his magnificent four volume *An Historical Syntax of the English Language,* traces the development and history of this troublesome combination of short words. He notes that some writers have posited that *it is me* arose in imitation of the French (*c'est moi* follows the same pattern of linking verb followed by objective pronoun) but points out that the earliest consistent use of *it is me* is several hundred years after the French language had its greatest impact on English. Visser's opinion is that it is likelier that *it is me* entered English on its own.

(He does provide a more detailed explanation, but it is highly unlikely that you will want to wade through it.)*

An Historical Syntax notes that *it is me* has been in increasing use since the end of the sixteenth century. The complaints against this type of use have been around for almost as long. This battle between the forces of correctness and the forces of usage makes the Hundred Years' War seem like a border skirmish. As far back as 1637 Ben Jonson stressed that "the verb am, that requireth the like case after it, as before it." Jonson himself was not always in the habit of putting his pronouns in agreement, as he was one of the earlier writers to use the dreaded phrase *between you and I.*†

The matter of the correctness of saying *it is I* or *it is me* has never had a uniformity of opinion. Grammarians in the eighteenth century frequently held opposing views on matters of linguistic propriety, as they struggled to come up with a rational explanation for the way the English language was used. Their views on *it is me* show this schism, as some, such as Joseph Priestley and Noah Webster, felt that it was quite reasonable to link the nominative *it* to the objective *me*. Most of their contemporaries did not share this view and continued to work against it.

But the efforts on the part of the grammarians to do away with *it is me* had little effect, and the phrase continued on its inexorable

----

* For those who do want to wade in, a slightly truncated version of Visser's argument is that *it is me* represents the "autochthonic development which English had in common with other Germanic languages . . . for the personal pronoun morpheme to develop two allomorphs: a) the unstressed, mostly proclitic one . . . and b) the stressed (oblique) ones . . . especially used when the pronoun stands more or less by itself, in the so-called disjunctive position." Don't say I didn't warn you.

† "Why, Macro, It hath beene otherwise, betweene you and I?" is found in Jonson's play *Sejanus.*

path forward. Over the course of the nineteenth century a great number of scholars on language had come to the conclusion that either it was perfectly reasonable to use *me*, or it might not be pretty, but it wasn't going away, so we might as well accept it. Another explanation given for why we are so prone to saying *it is me* is that the pronoun occurs in the part of the sentence where we generally would put the direct object, so it just feels right to us to use the objective case, rather than the nominative.

By the 1890s some writers were already of the opinion that not only was *it is me* acceptable but using *it is I* made one sound like a bit of a twerp. Barrett Wendell, is his 1891 book *English Composition*, asked "has not good use gone a long way to make *it is me* idiomatic, and *it is I* a bit pedantic? I do not feel at all sure that we can answer *No*."[58]

In the twentieth century, *me* and *I* continued their epic battle. A notable chapter occurred in 1921, when one Edward J. Tobin, superintendent of the schools in Cook County, Illinois, made a startling pronouncement: he directed the teachers in his district to stop correcting students who said "It is me." Tobin was the first prominent nonlinguist to say what many had been thinking: "What good does it do to teach school children a form of expression that is outlawed by common usage and by a sense of good form?"[59] The reaction was not a muted one.

"Murdering English" read the headline in the Columbia *Evening Missourian*. The article went on to say, "Mr. Tobin, by his action, helps to mutilate the language. He makes as his standard of speech the illiterate and goes to the gutter for his study."[60] Other newspapers had similar reactions: the Kentucky *Public Ledger* opted for the headline "Smashing English," and intoned, "What Mr. Tobin does when he throws down the mantle of this toleration over . . . the mutilation of the language involved in the barbarism

'It is me' is to take his standard of speech from the illiterate and to weaken all standards of clear and careful speech."[61]

Not to be outdone, the *Medicine Hat News* titled their article "Objectionable Usage," before offering what was perhaps the oddest complaint against the school administrator, sneering: "Superintendent Tobin is not even original in his contestation," as though the fact that he had made an observation that had been made before somehow diminished the strength of his argument.[62] There were a few newspapers who agreed with Tobin, some more so than others, but they were far outnumbered by his detractors. The furor was increased by the fact that Tobin had also stated that he would tell teachers to stop correcting students who used *he don't* in place of *he doesn't* or *he does not*.

Putting aside for the moment the question of whether Tobin was a brave man for his position on *it is me*, a foolish one for his position on *he don't*, or some combination therein, it is worth examining what the grammarians at this time were saying about *it is me*.

A Dictionary of Modern English Usage, written by Henry Fowler a mere five years after this imbroglio, held that using *me* in this way was "technically wrong" but didn't consider it much of a problem ("such a lapse is of no importance").[63] *Merriam-Webster's New International Dictionary* (published in 1909 and revised in 1921) said "This use of *me* violates the grammatical rule of construction which calls for a predicate nominative after *is*; and it is now chiefly colloquial or dialect, but is justified by some good writers as being historically idiomatic."[64] To be sure, there were still at this time plenty of usage guides that held that *it is me* was a mutilation of English, but there was a noticeable shift toward general acceptance.

Evidence of this shift may be found in Sterling Leonard's *Cur-*

rent English Usage, a monograph published by the National Coun-
cil of Teachers of English in 1932 that detailed the results of a
questionnaire on language use that had been sent to 229 judges.
The body of respondents was composed of "well known authors,
editors, business men, linguists, and teachers," with teachers
representing the largest portion. Regarding the propriety of *it is
me* only three of the twenty-eight linguists queried thought it was
illiterate; the rest viewed it as acceptable, in varying degrees.[65]

The fact that *it is me* continues to bother so many people
should not be taken as an indication that *it is I* is healthy and in
widespread use today. More likely is that it indicates that the condemnation of *it is me* is popular with a particular subgroup of
people (those who write to organizations with complaints). David
Crystal, writing about this in *The Cambridge Encyclopedia of the English Language,* noted that the great majority of people who complained about this in a BBC survey were over fifty, which makes
the list hardly representative of society at large.[66]

There is no aspect of the English language that has been im-
mune to change. Meanings and spellings shift, word order
changes, and punctuation comes and goes. The pronouns we use
today are markedly different from those used hundreds of years
ago, and continuing to rail against a pronoun that has achieved
widespread use can make one seem a bit imbalanced.

George Fox, the founder of the Religious Society of Friends,
serves as an example of this, in his 1660 book *A Battle-Door for
Teachers and Professors to Learn Singular & Plural.* Fox spent over a
hundred pages in explaining his view of the correct use of singular and plural pronouns. One of the reasons this took so long was
that his prose was copiously laden with insults directed toward
those he aimed to educate: "is he not a Novice and Unmannerly,
and an Ideot and a Fool, that speaks You to one, which is not to

be spoken to a singular, but to many? O Vulgar Professors and Teachers, that speaks Plural when they should Singular."[67] Fox's insistence that one should never use *you* when speaking to a single person had no effect on the language, save to earn him a footnote as one of our crankier language scolds.

What have we achieved, after almost four hundred years of telling speakers of English that they must match their nominatives? We have not eradicated *it is me*, which grows increasingly common. But it would be incorrect to say that these centuries of admonishments have had no effect at all: They have had one, but it is not the one intended. The confusion that came about from people being informed that *it is I* should be used rather than *it is me* assisted the rise of another kind of grammatical itching powder that has incensed sticklers for ages: *between you and I*.

BETWEEN YOU AND I

> I immediately asked Stein whether Williams had actually said "between he and I," and Harry solemnly confirmed the melancholy fact. The man who after Eugene O'Neill was our best playwright . . . had committed a grammatical error of unsurpassed grossness.
>
> —John Simon, *Paradigms Lost*, 1980

> All debts are cleared between you and I.
> —Shakespeare, *The Merchant of Venice*, 1600

Between you and I is not a recent construction. But it has seen increased use in the last few centuries as a result of innumerable speakers being tsked over their use of *it is me*. Many of these chastised speakers decided that the problem with their language use lay with the word *me*, and if they would only remove this offensive word all would be well. Hence, rather than say "between you and me," they chose to say "between you and I." This is commonly referred to as a hypercorrection.

A hypercorrection occurs when a speaker or writer creates a mistake by using what they think of as a more prestigious word. These typically are words that are correct in some other setting, just not the one that the speaker is using them in. Frequently *whom* will be forced into a sentence where *who* would work better, and the suffix -*ly* is unnecessarily tacked on to the end of a word.

Some scholars of language do not accept that *between you and I* represents a hypercorrected form of *between you and me*, on the grounds that the former has been in extensive English use since well before this whole mess became an issue. This seems plausible; people could not have been trying to correct their speech in this regard if it had not yet been established that it was a problem.

In addition to Shakespeare's famous use of it in *The Merchant of Venice*, this phrase appears in the writing of Ben Jonson, John Dryden, Henry Fielding, and numerous others. However, *between you and I* need not have been born of a single influence. It is certainly possible that one group of people used the expression in literary fashion, and some later group of people began to use it because they were sick of being corrected for saying *it is me*.

So *between you and I* had been trundling along in English usage since the beginning of the seventeenth century, well used by a large number of writers, until people suddenly began to take notice of it in the late eighteenth century and found it objectionable. Archibald Campbell used it in the first edition of his work *Lexiphanes*, published in 1767, and apparently received so much disparagement over this that when his book was reprinted he changed the wording to *between you and me* and added a footnote explaining some of the unkind things that had been said of him for using the offending *I*.[68]

Between you and I continued to be used throughout the nineteenth century, and it also continued to attract an increasing degree of scorn. Perhaps because English teachers and usage guides reserve their deepest scorn for the use of hypercorrections, there has been a remarkable degree of intransigence regarding *between you and I*.

Bryan Garner's *Modern English Usage*, which is one of the more flexible and thoughtful of the modern prescriptivist guides (he has a five-point scale for usage, ranging from "rejected" to "fully accepted"), labels it "widely shunned." In the 1975 edition of *Harper's Dictionary of Contemporary English*, 97 percent of the respondents on their usage panel voted against using this phrase in speech, and 98 percent said they would eschew it in writing.

This is a tricky issue for many people because it requires that one has either learned this grammatical rule well enough that it can be followed without any thought or it requires constant vigilance since using the nominative pronoun *I* would be correct in many similar circumstances. After all, if you can say "You and I both think Shakespeare is terrible" why can't you say "Between you and I, Shakespeare is terrible"?

Because the offending *I* in *between you and I* follows a preposition (*between*), and pronouns that follow prepositions are objects of it and so should be in the objective case. If it makes it easier to remember, you can try using a different preposition, such as *through*; saying, "We were playing basketball and he drove right through *I*" sounds quite wrong, while "he drove right through *me*" does not.

Some linguists have argued that there is a certain degree of historical precedent for accepting *between you and I*. The phrase, while fairly common in writing in the sixteenth and seventeenth centuries, shifted to occurring mainly in speech for much of the next two centuries, before being adopted again in writing as a hypercorrection. But the people who care about keeping objective and nominative pronouns in their proper place tend to be quite adamant about this matter and are unlikely to be swayed by an argument that is based on "If it's good enough for Shakespeare it's good enough for me."

I'M GOOD

Do not say "I feel good"; say "I feel well."
—A. Mortimer Clark and Jaxon Knox, *Progress in English*, 1931

"I Got You (I Feel Good)"
—James Brown song, 1965

Everyone has met the I'm-well corrector at some point or other. This is the person who asks, "How are you?," hears you respond, "I'm good," and then proceeds to make you feel less so by correcting your supposed error: "I think you meant to say 'I'm well.'"

Why do they do this? I don't mean to ask, "Why do these thinly smiling people always seize opportunities to denigrate the speech of others?," although that is a valid question. I mean, what is the reason such people believe the phrase "I'm good" is grammatically flawed? Specious grounds.

The logic behind this is that *good* is an adjective and since it follows a verb it should properly be an adverb. That sounds fine, so long as you avoid the basic way that English functions. The verb in question (*to be*) is another of those vile copulatives that we read about in "I vs. Me." Copulative, or linking, verbs can be followed by an adjective (what in this case in called a participle adjective).

Consider the following sentences: "I am irritated" and "You are annoying." In both cases we have a subject followed by a verb followed by an adjective—are these wrong? Of course not. Would the "I'm well" corrector change these to "I am irritatedly" and "I am annoyingly" in order to preserve the virtue of the adverb? Likely not.

Some people accept that an adjective can follow the linking verb here but insist that *good* is the wrong word for the job, and that *well* (which can be both adjective or adverb) is more properly suited to describing one's state of well-being. But the *Oxford English Dictionary* has attestations for *good* meaning "Of state of mind, courage, spirits: Not depressed or dejected" beginning in the twelfth century.[69] It functions quite well* as a way to describe one's state.

The proscription about using *good* for *well* came up first in the nineteenth century, when Richard Meade Bache condemned it in *Vulgarisms and Other Errors of Speech*. But the example that Bache used was the sentence, "He can do it as *good* as any one else can," in which case *good* would indeed be the wrong word. *Good* is here modifying the verb *do*, which is not a copulative verb. Numerous usage guides have warned against using the adjective *good* with such noncopulative verbs as "He threw the ball *good*." As a result of this, a number of people tarred all verbs with the "do not modify with *good*" brush.

There are arguments to be had regarding the use of *well* and

----

* Note that *well* was used here because it modifies the verb *function*, which is not a linking verb. One would not say "It functions quite *good* here."

good; some thoughtful people think that *well* should be used to describe one's state of physical health and *good* is more appropriate for describing one's mental state. I am afraid I don't observe such distinctions, but someone who engages you on this is deserving of a polite argument.

Not so the person who steadfast insists that *good* is improper in all cases when it follows a verb: They deserve your contempt. Respond to their correction as Joseph Welch did to Senator McCarthy during the latter's hearings on communist involvement in the U.S. Army: "Have you no sense of decency sir, at long last? Have you left no sense of decency?"

five

The Continuing Deterioration of the Language

In 1712, Jonathan Swift published *A Proposal for Correcting, Improving, and Ascertaining the English Tongue,* in the form of a letter to Robert Harley, the first Earl of Oxford. Swift was highly excited about the terrible state the English language was in, and appealed to Harley to assist him in establishing an academy, modeled after the one in France, that would guard the English language.

Swift repeatedly warned about the danger that English was in and found multiple ways that it could be improved. According to him, "our Language is extremely imperfect; that its daily Improvements are by no means in proportion to its daily Corruptions; and the Pretenders to polish and refine it, have chiefly multiplied Abuses and Absurdities; and, that in many Instances, it offends against every Part of Grammar."[1]

The opinions of Swift were not uncommon. Many others had

had similar feelings before him, and to this day we are routinely warned that the English language is under siege. One would think that centuries of pronouncements of doom unaccompanied by any actual loss of ability to communicate would give some measure of comfort. Such has not been the case.

Little has changed since Swift's day. Many of us are still fixated on the idea that the English language was slowly but surely getting better and better, improving itself with night classes and a good diet, but that at some recent point things took a dramatic turn for the worse.

Relax. English is not dying. It is behaving exactly as it should, which is to say it is changing. All living languages change—it is one of the things that indicate that they are still in use by a large number of people. The problem is that, while many people accept that our language is subject to change, they want to dictate what sort of changes will take place and that is a very difficult thing to do.

If we had not corrupted our language we would still be addressing each other with *thee* and *thou*, and nobody wants that. Following is a sampling of the daily corruptions that our language has been subjected to.

'!
_____

His (that is, *He's*) *Her's, Our's, Your's, Their's*, have evidently the Form of the Possessive Case.
    —Robert Lowth, *A Short Introduction to English Grammar*, 1763

The possessive pronouns, without a substantive, should be used without the apostrophe.
    —J. Mennye, *An English Grammar*, 1785

Whatever quibble one may have with Kingsley Amis's* views on both the subjects of drinking and grammar, one must admit that he had a memorable ability to turn a phrase when describing either. In terms of the former, he authored perhaps the single greatest description of a hangover, writing in *Lucky Jim*: "His mouth had been used as a latrine by some small creature of the night, and then as its mausoleum."

Amis was no less felicitous in describing certain aspects of grammar, and his succinct and pessimistic take on the apostrophe, and the difficulties it presents to so many, is masterful: "The rules governing the use of this vexing little mark are evidently hard to master, and if you have any trouble with them or it after the age of fourteen or so, the chances are that you will always be liable to error in the matter."[2]

I suspect that many people who read books such as this view the world as composed of two forever distinct groups of people: those who do know how to use an apostrophe and those who do not. This "stepchild of English orthography"† gives them a useful measure with which to judge whether or not a person is someone with whom they would care to have their children associate.

The misuse of the apostrophe is something that is also frequently held up as evidence that the English language is in a state of decline, as it is often maintained that the ability to wield it correctly has diminished. This position presupposes that there

---

* At various points in the past few hundred years, the genitive form of Amis could have been written *Amis', Amises, Amis's, Amis,* and *Amis his.* I have adopted the modern form.

† In the words of Elizabeth S. Sklar, the author of "The Possessive Apostrophe," p. 175, a fine treatise on the history of the apostrophe, and one that I recommend to anyone who wishes to learn more of its history.

has at some point been a utopian period of English, during which we all used our apostrophes just so, and offenders had their thumbs cut off and were forced to wear the digits hung around their necks as apostrophic-shaped marks of shame. This, however, is very far from the truth, for this simple and diminutive curve has bedeviled both those who would regulate and those who would simply use it ever since its first use.

First of all, where did the apostrophe come from? Opinion of the origins of what Donald Hook called a "printer's gimmick"[3] are, like almost everything else about the apostrophe, mixed. There seems to be speculation that it was first introduced into print in 1509, in an edition of Petrarch.[4] Others hold that it was first used in 1529 by Geoffroy Tory, a prominent French printer, who was also responsible for the introduction of the cedilla and the accent. In order to hedge their bets, most people who have written about the early history of the apostrophe (all three or four of them) say that it was "promoted" (or some such word) by Tory.

Following Tory's promotion of the apostrophe, it was found occasionally in French printed works and made its first appearance in an English text in 1559, in the *Cosmographical Glasse*, by William Cunningham. The apostrophe was first used as a mark of elision, or contraction, signifying that one or more letters had been omitted from the word to which it was attached. We are all familiar with this practice and most of us have no trouble with writing words such as *did not* as *didn't*, or *I have* as *I've*. We even take easily to somewhat illogical contractions, such as *won't* for *will not*.

This portion of the apostrophe's history is all relatively cut-and-dried. After that it gets rather confusing.

First, there was no real agreement as to what letters were replaced by the apostrophe. Sometimes it replaced an *e* that didn't really need to be there, in such forms as *damn'd* or *th'*. Other times it would replace letters such as the (mostly) silent *l* in *would*, *could*, and *should*. It soon took on greater duties, replacing larger portions of words such as the *wi-* in *I will*, and the *re* and *as* in *fo'c'sle*.* The *Merriam-Webster Dictionary of English Usage* notes some examples of other words that suffered by apostrophes under the Restoration dramatists, including some that we would hardly recognize as words at all today: *i'fac*, *'zbud*, *dar'st* (presumably contractions of *in fact*, *god's blood*, and *darest*).

There were some who complained about this bit of punctuation in its infancy, but by and large the use of apostrophe as elision settled into acceptance as a necessary part of English writing. However, trouble was not long in coming, for soon the mark took on a new role: designating the genitive, or possessive, case. This began at the end of the sixteenth century, but was not widespread for some while. As the *Oxford Companion to the English Language* notes, the First Folio of Shakespeare, published in 1623, only used them in 4 percent of the instances of possessives that would typically have such a mark today.[5]

Further confusing the issue, there has been considerable disagreement as to what exactly the apostrophe was doing in its genitive role. One thought was that it was simply functioning again as a contraction as there was a common habit of writing possessives such as "the man his child," which would then become "the man's child." George Harris, in his *Observations upon the English Language* (1752), wrote "The Letter *s* frequently stands for *his*: for

----

* The word in question is written forecastle in full, and it refers to the forward-most part of a ship's upper deck, where the crew typically is quartered.

Example—We say The King's Majesty, instead of the King his Majesty,"[6] although he took pains to note that he disliked the practice. There was mixed opinion as to the origins and correctness of inserting the possessive *his* into the language in this fashion. Many thought it was simply a mistake that was picked up by writers (including Shakespeare).

This was not a view shared by all. Charles Peter Mason, a nineteenth-century grammarian, said of this notion: "The mistake is so stupid, and shows such blank ignorance of the principles of grammar, that one wonders how the notion could have originated."[7] Yet others were of the opinion that it was a common, and not mistaken, usage. Furthermore, George Krapp, in his 1909 book *Modern English*, asserts that the *his* was not spoken out loud, and functioned almost exactly as would the genitive *s*.[8]

This theory of an elliptical *his* is not widely subscribed to anymore; a more plausible one is that while the apostrophe used as a genitive marker is indeed a contraction, it functions in a different way; one that reflects on the Old English roots of our language.

A common inflection of the singular genitive masculine and neuter nouns in Old English was simply to add -*es* to a word. The word for king, *cyning*, became *cyninges* in its genitive form. As Old English became Middle English feminine nouns began to likewise inflect their genitive singular cases. Following this line of reasoning, the apostrophe stands in for the soon to be missing *e*.

Initially, the genitive apostrophe was only used in the case of singular nouns; the rules governing what to do with apostrophes for the genitive plural came later, and after a good deal of turmoil. In fact, the grammarians of the eighteenth century had little agreement about how the apostrophe should be used in any of its genitive roles. Some thought that it worked for pronouns as well as nouns, averring that *her's* and *it's* were just fine. Others thought it should be used for some definite pronouns but not for indefinite ones. Still others had a jumbled combination of thoughts on this, as many of them changed their minds from one edition of their published grammars to the next. There was a similar confusion about how to use it for plural genitives as well.

In the eighteenth century, the apostrophic wars raged unyielding to any temporal or moral boundaries. Families were rent asunder, nations split, and an entire generation came of age not knowing how exactly they should mark their genitive cases or indicate a contraction. The last part is true, at least if you count the rather small percentage of the population who knew how to spell—the rest of the population paid no attention to all this. And even among the educated, most didn't really care. But the grammarians had a fine time of it, contradicting each other and trying to create some sense of order without having to rely overmuch on common sense.

Some grammarians were in favor of using an apostrophe to mark plural nouns, especially if they ended with a vowel. Others thought that this was nonsense, saying everyone knows that the apostrophe is only for marking ellipsis. Yet others thought that either sounded just fine and had no dog in the genitive/plural fight, and instead they reserved all their energies for fighting about what pronouns should use an apostrophe.

Again, there was no agreement here—some thought that no pronouns should have apostrophes, except one or two, maybe, like *who's* or *one's*. Some liked the look of *it's* for the genitive and hated the way it looked when *it is* tried to put it on, and some felt just the reverse.

It must be noted that the question of how one should indicate the genitive form of something was not confined to the prospects of adding an *s* or an *'s*. In 1586, William Bullokar, a schoolteacher, spelling reform advocate,* and author of the first English grammar, published a short work that was intended to serve as an abbreviated companion to his grammar. The title was *William Bullokarz Pamphlet for Grammar*. The full title contained the words *"Hiz Abbreviation of Hiz Grammar for English, Extracted Out-of Hiz Grammar at-Larg,"* so while it is possible that Bullokar intended the *z* to indicate possession, it also seems likely that he just preferred it to using an *s*.

It is easy to look back on the convoluted and seemingly arbitrary uses of the apostrophe in centuries gone by and laugh at the ways that it was misused. Surely, we say to ourselves, we have finally worked this thing out. We have a concrete set of rules that we may apply and if only people would sit up and pay attention in class we would be forever spared the gruesome sight of storefront windows advertising "Cucumber's—$.59/lb."

But we haven't yet worked out all the kinks, and even today the role of the apostrophe is in flux. Several decades ago it was common to write the numerical form of decades with an apostrophe (as in *1980's*), a practice that is now fading. And a number of stores, particularly in Britain, no longer use the genitive apostrophe in brand names, so that *Harrod's* is now written as *Harrods*. The apostrophe will doubtless continue to squirm and shift in the years to come. So try to remember, the next time you find gorge

---

* The editors of the *Oxford Dictionary of National Biography*, with their typical wit, conclude the entry on Bullokar by writing, "It is a pity that such a dedicated scholar should have spent so much time and effort on the reform of English orthography, which has remained to this day a lost cause."

rising in your throat over a misplaced or needless apostrophe, that what you are witnessing may be nothing more than the continuing evolution of a part of English punctuation that has never known peace and stability.

So in lieu of any formal pronouncement of rules, here is what I hope will be a helpful list of the many roles of the apostrophe and how it should, and should not, be used (at least according to various grammar guides of the past several hundred years).

1. It functions as a contraction, indicating that one or more letters are missing. Except when the letters aren't actually missing, as when the seventeenth-century poet Robert Herrick wrote "What fate decreed, time now ha's made us see."*

2. It indicates possession in singular nouns, sitting between the end of the noun and an *s*. Except when it didn't, as in the case of names that already end in an *s*, such as *Jones' book* (a practice that is now out of style). Or when it comes at the end of certain words that end in a sibilant, such as *for conscience' sake*.

3. It indicates possession for plural nouns, between the end of the plural word and the *s* that follows, as in *children's*. Except when the word ends in an *s*, in which case it should come at the end of the word, with no additional *s* added ("the books' covers").

- - - - - - - - - - - - - - - - - -

* "To Prince Charles Upon His Coming to Exeter." As Barbara Strang has noted, this was a not uncommon way of writing *has*.

4. It does not indicate possession for pronouns, which are written as *hers*, *theirs*, and *ours*. Except when it does, for certain indefinite pronouns, such as *A Room of One's Own*.

5. *It's* should be used only to mean *it is* and should never be used to indicate the third-person neuter possessive pronoun, unless you are an idiot (such as Thomas Jefferson*).

6. It is widely acknowledged that apostrophes should never be used with verbs. Except when they should: Jeremiah Wharton, in his 1654 *English Grammar*, held that the third-person singular (as in "He write's very poorly") should use an apostrophe.[9] This view appears to have been unique to Wharton; no other grammarians have made such a claim.

7. The apostrophe should not be used to indicate the plural of a noun. Except when it does. It formerly fulfilled this function for some plural nouns, especially of a foreign origin, that would end in a vowel (such as *folio's*), as well as for some plural nouns that would end in a sibilant sound (such as *waltz's*). Until recently it was used to indicate the plural form of decades (*1980's*), numbers (*6's* and *7's*), individual letters written as plurals (*dot your*

- - - - - - - - - - - - - - - - - -

* Jefferson, and many other eighteenth-century writers, commonly used an apostrophe for both forms of *it's*. In a letter to William Short on July 1, 1790, he wrote "It is to receive it's third reading to-day, and tho' it depends on a single vote, yet I believe we may count surely that it will pass that house."

i's and cross your t's), abbreviations (*BMOC's* and *VIP's*), and symbols (*#'s* and *&'s*).

I trust that this will clear up any confusion on the matter.

George Bernard Shaw, brave and contrarian soul that he was, refused to use apostrophes in contractions, unless to do otherwise would create confusion. It may be tempting to throw in the towel and follow Shaw's lead here, but you would be emulating the language instincts of a man who left a substantial amount of money in his will to fund the creation of a new alphabet to make spelling easier.

One point for any readers finding themselves over Amis's decreed fourteen years of age and fearing themselves unable to ever grasp the finer points of how to properly wield an apostrophe: Should you find yourself ever subjected to the taunts of a grammarian who insists on pointing out that you have abused this punctuation mark, you may always fall back on the time-honored tradition of grammarians everywhere and attack your attacker.

For it should be noted that almost everyone, even those who are most punctilious about its placement, are pronouncing the word *apostrophe* in a manner that was formerly considered incorrect. The entry on *apostrophe* found in the second edition of the *Oxford English Dictionary* provides an editorial aside for this, noting that "It ought to be of three syllables in English as in French," noting that the word "has been ignorantly confused" with the pronunciation of another form of apostrophe (a rhetorical figure of speech). The French pronunciation is *ah-poss-TROFF.*

POTATO(E)

> Potato
>> —William Figueroa, writing on blackboard for spelling bee at Muñoz Rivera Elementary School, June 15, 1992

> Spell that . . . spell that again now. Add one little bit on the end . . . I think it's *potatoe*.
>> —James Danforth Quayle, addressing William Figueroa on June 15, 1992

Some people may well find it odd that a book on any aspect of the English language should contain within its pages a full-throated defense of Dan Quayle. Yet not only will I defend our oft-maligned forty-fourth vice president, I will make the case that Quayle has done more to effect proper English spelling than anyone reading this book.

Everyone who was born at least ten years before 1992 knows two things: that *potato* has no *e* at the end of it, and that Dan Quayle mistakenly insisted that it does, in a spectacularly public fashion, when he attempted to correct a fifth-grader at a spelling bee in June of that year. Since then, Quayle has become synonymous with poor spelling, to the extent that almost twenty years after the incident, his son Ben was still being teased for his father's error, when Quayle fils was running for elective office.*

----

* A column by Gail Collins in the *New York Times* of August 11, 2010, on the prospects of Ben Quayle running for Congress contained the line: "Well, the apple doesn't fall far from the tree. Or the potatoe."

I am not concerned with whether Quayle was correct or not—he was obviously wrong in his spelling, at least as far as the overlords of spelling bees are concerned—but I am concerned with the question of why we all know that *potato* has no *e* at the end of it. The answer to this question is that many of us now have a firm grasp of this thanks to our beleaguered former vice president. In other words, Dan Quayle died for your sins.

This statement requires a bit of explanation. To be sure, there is some portion of the English-speaking and -spelling population for whom the correct spelling of this tuber was never in doubt. Those worthies who can type *embarrassment, misspell,* and *liaison* without a moment's hesitation or even a glance at the spell-check all knew immediately that Quayle had erred, and they should feel secure in the heartwarming contempt they allowed to seep through their souls when they heard of it. But what of the rest of us, the vast majority of the population who have spent large amounts of our adult lives carrying about some small degree of dread that we've used an *i* when we should have used an *e*? Why do we all know that *potato* has no *e* at the end?

Potato entered the English language in the middle of the sixteenth century, according to the *Oxford English Dictionary*. In addition to providing examples of a word's usage over the centuries, the *OED* also provides any variant spellings that have had currency, and *potato* has had quite a few. There have been no fewer than sixty-four different ways of spelling *potato* over the past 450 years, and that's counting only the ones that begin with *p* (there have been an additional four variants beginning with *b*). We have eaten *patattos, potawtoes, purtatoes, potaaties, pottytus,* and seemingly innumerable other olios of p's, t's, and vowels.

Almost all of these are regionalisms or archaic spellings that have long since died out, but there is one that has had surprising

longevity, appearing in print throughout almost all of the twentieth century—the humble *potatoe.*

An article in the paper of record, the mighty *New York Times,*
published on September 16, 1988, refers to a "bland carrot-and-
potatoe puree." The following year, on November 22, 1989, one
can find a caption to a photo in the *Washington Post* describing
the "sweet potatoe and pumpkin pies."

Continuing to the next decade, an article in the *San Francisco
Chronicle,* January 23, 1991, is boldly headlined "One Potatoe
More," with no apparent sense of incipient irony. Perhaps oddest
of all, an editorial in the *Salt Lake Tribune* from May 28, 1992,
around two weeks before Quayle's spelling bee debacle, contains
the line: "Slowly the terrible implications dawned on Clyde
Fernwilter—could he be rendered irrelevant by a genetically
superior couch potatoe?"

It does not seem that any of these errant *e*'s drew howls of
protest down on the heads of the ombudsmen or editors of any
of these fine newspapers. So why has there been near-universal
opprobrium heaped upon Quayle? The fact that he was widely
viewed as an intellectual lightweight doubtless has much to do
with it, but there is also a marked inclination in modern U.S.
politics for those on the left to make fun of the linguistic capa-
bilities (or perceived lack) of those on the right.

George W. Bush received almost as much ridicule as Quayle
for his use of the word *misunderestimate,* yet no similar treatment
has been afforded to John Conyers Jr. (a famous, and famously
liberal, congressman) who, when speaking to the Department of
Agriculture, said "If you misunderestimate the power of the in-
tense bureaucracy in these agencies and departments and federal
institutions, you go, they stay." This was in 1997, three years before
Bush said "They misunderestimated me." And political leanings

are certainly part of the uproar over Sarah Palin's unfortunate blend of *refuse* and *repudiate*, in which she tweeted the message "Peaceful Muslims, pls refudiate" in 2010 (see page 57). This coinage, while not terribly common, has been in occasional use for well over a hundred years and was never viewed as indicative of a grave intellectual failing.

Had Quayle the benefit of studying the misspellings of his forebears, he would have had plenty of ammunition with which to refute his critics. He might have looked down his nose at those orthographically rabid jackals of the press and murmured something along the lines of "I'm sorry, I was spelling the word in the same manner employed by the second vice president of our country . . . perhaps you've heard of him? An unlearned fellow by the name of Thomas Jefferson."*

If Quayle wanted to cite past presidents as evidence for his refutation of the fifth-grader, he would have had an even more impressive roster to draw from. George Washington,[10] James Madison,[11] Andrew Jackson,[12] Ulysses S. Grant,[13] and James Garfield[14] all have writings published with this grievous error. Even Franklin Delano Roosevelt, who has rarely been called an idiot, was unable to resist the siren call of that silent *e*, when he wrote a letter to his parents while a student at Groton, informing them that "the 1st heat of the potatoe race was run today."[15]

Yet we never hear of any of them tarred with the same brush as Quayle, even though all of these presidents have had healthy numbers of detractors. One never hears "George Washington had

----

* The polymath of Monticello certainly did not always spell *potato* thusly, but in a letter to Horatio Spafford on May 14, 1809, he wrote "I presume you speak of the Irish potatoe."

a terrible temper, and also had trouble spelling *potato*." Or "Ulysses S. Grant was a drunk, and couldn't spell worth spit." Why not?

The first, and most obvious reason, is that spellings change over time, and many of these presidents were writing about *potatoes* at a time before the "correct" spelling became entirely codified. But no less important a reason is that there were far more substantive things about all these men to take issue with. Taunting someone whose political leanings you disagree with over the issue of whether they can spell a commonly misspelled word makes as much sense as teasing them for the color of their socks.

Quayle was not the only American political figure to run into trouble with orthography on the campaign trail. In 1882, George Hearst, the famous mining magnate and father of William Randolph, was running for the governorship of California, on the Democratic ticket. He was widely derided for his perceived lack of education, and in an attempt to quiet his critics, he gave a speech with one of the most pragmatic takes on spelling I have ever heard: "My opponents say that I haven't the book learning that they possess. They say I can't spell. They say I spell bird, b-u-r-d. If b-u-r-d doesn't spell bird, what in hell does it spell?"[16] Hearst's logic, while impeccable, was not enough to convince voters, and he lost the election.

In summation, *potato* is now a word that is spelled incorrectly far less frequently than it was a few decades ago since no one wants to bring upon themselves the comparison to Dan Quayle. And for that we all owe the vice president a debt of gratitude.

OMG, ☺

> With the necessity to abbreviate and digitalize in rapid fire, spelling and grammar become unnecessary and a lost art. This is reflected in our students' low reading and writing levels. With abbreviations such as LOL and OMG, our language skills diminish. Our divided attention causes accidents, unawareness of our surroundings and identity fraud.
>
> —Dick Cory, letter to *Chico Enterprise-Record* newspaper,
> March 4, 2013

> OMG!!! OED!!! LOL!!!!!
> —*New York Times* editorial headline, April 4, 2011

We love writers who refuse to be shackled by the confines of language; brave men and women who wrestle English to the ground and turn it to their own ends. James Joyce was famous for the chimeric linguistic combinations dotting his work. Thomas Urquhart, the Scottish poet, was responsible for coining such common words as *capsule* and *horrific* as well as less common specimens such as *plutomania* (a frenzied pursuit of wealth) and *bumdockdousse* (a game, now infrequently played, which appears to entail little more than three people standing about and kicking each other in the buttocks). We frequently hear of Shakespeare's genius, with the fact that he purportedly invented one-tenth of the twenty thousand or so words in his vocabulary offered as evidence of this genius. We extol these writers for their ability to breathe new life into English. How odd then, that we should not extend this same courtesy to today's youth.

Complaining about the linguistic proclivities of teenagers is about as predictable as complaining about their choice in music, and for their part, teenagers appear to care about your opinion of their language choice and musical tastes in equal measure (which is to say, not at all). With the recent introduction of new methods of communicating (such as email, texting, and instant messaging), the concerns regarding young people's deleterious effect on English have reached a fevered pitch. One indication of this may be found in the scorn that is heaped upon many of the initialisms found in textspeak.*

Abbreviated forms of speech are not new, by any means, but their use has enjoyed a renaissance of late. This is owing to the typographic design that was initially employed in the keyboard of mobile telephones, in which a mere ten keys served to provide almost all of the characters in a missive, as well as the fact that messages sent via mobile phone or instant messaging are generally brief communications. They tend to be almost colloquial forms of writing, rather than carefully composed letters. Quick and dirty works just fine, hence the proliferation of *brb*, *LOL*, and perhaps worst of all: *OMG*.

But are these ugly little conglomerates of letters really destroying the ability of youth to communicate? And are they even new? In the case of *OMG*, it is not very new at all.

In March 2011, the *Oxford English Dictionary* elicited some cries of protest when it announced that it was including *OMG* as part of its ongoing revision of the dictionary. However, what many of the critics did not do was look at the evidence provided by this

----

* For those of you who care about such things, there is a difference between an acronym and an initialism. The former refers to an abbreviation consisting of letters that are pronounced as a single word (such as NASA), and the latter refers to an abbreviation consisting of letters that are pronounced separately (such as CIA).

dictionary—it was not merely reproducing the febrile thumb work of one slack-jawed thirteen-year-old to another.

The first recorded use to date of *OMG* is from 1917, and reads in full "I hear that a new order of Knighthood is on the tapis—O.M.G. (Oh! My God!)—Shower it on the Admiralty!" The citation comes from a letter by one John Arbuthnot Fisher, who happens to have been the admiral in charge of the British navy (a position known as first sea lord), and was written to Winston Churchill, staunch defender of both the English people and their language. One can hardly make the case that this use of *OMG* represents the decline of the English language and civilization. What of other such initialed specimens?

Some of these instances of shorthand, such as *LOL, brb, TMI,* are in fact of recent vintage. However, as has been pointed out by David Crystal* and others, many of the examples commonly found in textspeak predate texting itself by a considerable margin. Crystal makes the case that much of textspeak shares elements with rebuses, those cryptic representations of words that have been used for thousands of years. Even if one disagrees with him as to whether textspeak bears any resemblance to this kind of puzzle, there is no doubt that much of the telephone shorthand has been in use for a long time.†

Much of the opposition to textspeak appears to have more to do with the circumstances surrounding its use than with the ac-

----

* Crystal, a professor of linguistics and the author of over a hundred books on the English language, published an examination of textspeak in 2008 titled *Txtng: the gr8 db8.*

† Edward Courtenay's *Dictionary of Abbreviations*, published in 1855, states that "U is sometimes used to express the pronoun *you.*"

tual concept of communicating a phrase or sentiment through abbreviation. After all, there is very little inherent difference between *brb* and *RIP*, except that the latter has been used as a memorial for over four hundred years, and the former has been used for the past twenty to indicate that a computer user with whom one is chatting is going to the bathroom. The English language has long been awash in these initialisms, which range from the formal (*QED*) to the colloquial (*aka*) to the scientific (*REM*).

There is also a historical precedent for this type of abbreviated writing, found in forms of jargon particular to specific fields, such as the writing done in courts of law and in the language used to write telegrams and cables. Since people had to pay by the word, such missives were extremely brief; many people used telegram dictionaries, which were essentially long lists of code words, each one of which stood for some complete thought or sentence.*

A number of English books for students in the early twentieth century included instructions for how to properly shorten telegrams, by removing unnecessary letters from words. A paper published in the *English Journal* in 1931 outlining a sample lesson plan for high school English makes note of the need to learn how to shorten words for this purpose.[17] In the days when Western Union was the great facilitator of communication, we were teaching high school children how to write in textspeak.

But even if one comes to accept that the initialisms and acronyms found in textspeak are a natural part of language, surely there must be some portion of electronic communication that we

----

* In an 1876 edition of the *ABC Universal Commercial Electric Telegraphic Code*, the code word *daintiness* translated to "sustained other considerable damage" and *anciently* stood for "What appliance have you got for lifting heavy machinery?"

can safely point to as indication of intellectual decline. Perhaps those horrid little aberrations of punctuation that people put together in emails and texts, the emoticon.* Are these entirely the province of unimaginative youth? Sadly, no—the emoticon is far older than even the oldest, most curmudgeonly critic who rails against their use.

They may have flourished more of late, but emoticons came of age when Rutherford B. Hayes occupied the White House. The first recorded use of an emoticon is found in the writings of Ambrose Bierce, the splenetic author of such works as *The Devil's Dictionary* and *Write It Right: A Handbook of Literary Faults*. In 1887, Bierce suggested the use of what he referred to as a "snigger point" (thought to be either _/ or a parenthesis drunkenly lying on its side) to represent a mouth, and denoting jocular or ironic sentiments.[18]

Bierce was not exactly the first person to create an emoticon; they appeared slightly earlier in the decade, when *Puck* magazine had a small article, titled "Typographical Art," which provided four illustrations of human emotion, as rendered in type. They were joy, melancholy, indifference, and astonishment. There does not appear to have been any intention that they should actually be used in writing.

Since the notion that the emoticon came from the celebrated author of an English usage guide may be a hard pill for some to swallow, it may make it easier to accept their existence knowing that Vladimir Nabokov also was in favor of these typographic excreta, telling an interviewer in 1974 that he often thought "there should exist a special typographical sign for a smile."

- - - - - - - - - - - - - - - - - -

* Emoticons are representations of facial expressions intended to convey emotion; you may think of them as minuscule typographic gargoyles.

Texting and instant messaging are conversations that just happen to take place in written form. They are not intended to represent language that should be recorded for the ages any more than the conversation you have with a deli clerk about your coffee or the spat you have with your significant other about the groceries someone forgot to get. Textspeak and emoticons are an attempt to inject some life into a fairly lifeless medium and are deserving of more than a blanket condemnation.

AIN'T

> [A]in't is a barbarism, because it never has been in good use.
> —Philo Melvin Buck and William Schuyler,
> *The Art of Composition; For High Schools and Academies,* 1907

> I ain't vexed at this puppy business of the bishops, although I was a little at first.
> —Jonathan Swift, November 24, 1710

There has likely been no word more subject to linguistic hand-wringing than the humble little *ain't*. It has been the subject of countless polemics written to editors, of study in academic papers, and furiously whispered corrections to children: "*Ain't* is not a word!" There are only two things that appear to be certain about *ain't*: its use has been widely condemned, and it has flourished in spite of this condemnation. The rest remains a mystery.

Ain't is obviously a contracted form of multiple English words, but no one knows for certain what those words are. It may be "am not I," "are not I," or some other combination of verb, pronoun, and apostrophe. It is uncertain also at what point it first entered

The Continuing Deterioration of the Language   143

the language or what form preceded it. It is generally held that it was formerly used as *an't* and before that was *a'n't*.

Perhaps reading this causes you to brightly sit up in your chair and think that by simply staring at this word for a few thoughtful minutes you can puzzle out what these contractions stood for. Maybe you will receive acclaim for being the first person to conclusively decipher the roots of *ain't*. Feel free to do so, but be advised that many thoughtful people, academics tweedy and otherwise, have spent considerable time attempting the same thing, and no one yet has come up with a theory that has had a broad consensus in its favor.

Ain't provides a splendid example of prescriptivist success: It sounds wrong to us because we have been told it is wrong. But there is nothing more wrong about *ain't* than a number of other seemingly illogical contractions that we use without a second thought.

In 1961, when the Merriam-Webster company published their *Third New International Dictionary*, it contained the following note for *ain't*: "though disapproved by many and more common in less educated speech, used orally in most parts of the U.S. by many cultivated speakers esp. in the phrase *ain't I*."[19] The uproar that met publication of this dictionary, spurred in large part by the perceived approval of *ain't*, was severe enough that three separate books have been published on the subject.*

----

* The first was *Dictionaries and That Dictionary*, a series of essays edited by James Sledd and Wilma Ebbitt. This is sadly out of print, but worth buying secondhand, especially for those who are interested in an academic approach. Following this was Herbert Morton's *Story of Webster's Third*. Published in 1995, this provides an excellent overview of the controversy and a general history of the Merriam-Webster company. And in 2012 David Skinner published *The Story of Ain't*, an utterly captivating book that places the story of this dictionary within the American cultural climate of the time.

Among the more notable critics were Dwight Macdonald, whose 1962 essay in the *New Yorker* ("The String Untuned") was seen by many as the most devastating critique of the dictionary. In his review, Macdonald said that he regretted "that the nineteenth-century schoolteachers without justification deprived us of *ain't* for *am not*"[20] but still thought "the deed is done" and the word should be marked dialectical or illiterate. Garry Wills opened his review of the dictionary in the *National Review* with the lines "The large new Merriam-Webster has all the modern virtues. It is big, expensive and ugly. It should be a great success."[21] Wills found little to favor in the dictionary and sarcastically commented "only an oppressor of the poor would even suggest that 'ain't' is not a desirable addition to any man's vocabulary."

These writers had something in common in addition to their dislike of Merriam-Webster's dictionary and its treatment of *ain't*: They both used the offending word themselves, in very much the way that the dictionary described how people used it.

Macdonald's use of *ain't* can be found in a letter he wrote: "I've always thought . . . that when I get old (as now—67 ain't no chicken) I'd like to review my past as preserved in letters from and to me."[22] And in Wills's *Nixon Agonistes* we find the line "Now the reporter asked Rockefeller to say it ain't so. Rockefeller said it ain't so."[23] Some critics of the dictionary held that, while "cultivated speakers" might use *ain't*, they really only did so in a jocular fashion. But it has not yet been established that jocular use of language does not count.

Ain't is deeply enshrined in our cultural consciousness. We find it in song titles (*Ain't She Sweet*; *It Don't Mean a Thing* [*If It Ain't Got That Swing*]) and commonly used phrases ("Say it ain't so, Joe"; "Ain't that a kick in the head/teeth/etc.," "politics ain't bean-bag"). And it is no less enshrined in our canon of disapproved words; it is the word that we all know is thought of lowly and which we use for effect.

The makers of Webster's Third had been unfairly criticized regarding their inclusion of *ain't*. For one thing, they were not the first to define this word in a dictionary: Merriam-Webster had been including the word since 1890, as had many other dictionaries. Additionally, asking the makers of a dictionary to somehow do away with the impurities of the language makes no more sense than asking the editors of a biology textbook to do away with an animal or a virus one does not care for. Both merely record the life forms they see, they do not regulate them. The makers of Webster's Third were not, as some averred, giving their seal of approval to the word *ain't*; they were simply noting that it was being used.

If you so hate this word that you must actively campaign against it, you should reserve your opprobrium for the people who use the word (including Wills and Macdonald with their less literate brethren), rather than the people who simply catalog its use.

LEG VS. LIMB

There exists an affected or prudish use of the word *limb* instead of *leg*, when leg is meant, which cannot be too severely censured. Such squeamishness is absurd.
—Frank Vizetelly, *A Desk Book of Errors in English*, 1907

I well remember reproving a young lady but recently from France, and a novice in the English language, from saying "leg" in company, telling her she must say limb. A few minutes after she called her arm her limb. I told her that was unnecessary, she might say arm but not leg.
—E. S. McKee, *Virginia Medical Monthly*, February 1891

There are a number of words that we use freely today that would have once occasioned reactions ranging from a raised eyebrow to a slap. These citizens of the English language have shed their pejorative usage labels and are no longer considered vulgar. Words such as *fubar** and *scumbag*† have become sufficiently mainstream that they are often found in the pages of daily newspapers.

For some who remember when these words were considered wholly inappropriate it can sound jarring to hear them bandied about in polite conversation and may seem to lend credence to the notion that English is today in a state of decline. Yet this process of words that are considered offensive becoming gentrified and entering into widespread use is not new, and the way that we have treated words for certain body parts provides a fine example of how our feelings about some words can change. I am referring, of course, to the unspeakable word *leg*.

Frederick Marryat was a British novelist and naval officer who spent several years traveling in North America and published an account of his travels in a book titled *A Diary in America, with Remarks on its Institutions* (1839). One of the institutions he remarked on was the curious habit Americans had of employing euphemisms. Marryat wrote "There are certain words which are never used in America, but an absurd substitute is employed."[24] He then told a story about how he had managed to mortally offend a young woman through his use of the word *leg* and was informed that the polite word to use would have been *limb*. Marryat

----

* *Fubar* was originally formed as an acronym, meaning "fucked up beyond all recognition."

† The original meaning of *scumbag* referred to a used condom and was considered quite a bit more vulgar than it is today.

also reported that the American aversion to legs extended beyond mentioning the word, as he witnessed a boarding school piano that had all of its limbs dressed in "modest little trousers, with frills at the bottom of them!"[25]

Even Richard Grant White, who rarely met a usage that he didn't want to proscribe against, found this preposterous, writing of *limb*, "A squeamishness, which I am really ashamed to notice, leads many persons to use this word exclusively instead of *leg*."[26] White continued, "Perhaps these persons think that it is indelicate for a woman to have legs, and that therefore they are concealed by garments, and should be ignored in speech. Heaven help such folk; they are far out of my reach."[27] If you are stricter about language use than Richard Grant White, a man who wrote an entire chapter titled "Words That Are Not Words" and who was roundly mocked by even his fellow language scolds for his prescriptiveness, then you should just stop listening to people's language altogether since you will always be unhappy with the way that it is used.

White was not the only usage writer to make note of this distinction. In *Vulgarisms and Other Errors of Speech*, Richard Meade Bache wrote "An Englishman, to whom an American woman should say, 'I have the rheumatism in one of my limbs,' might inquire, 'Which?' if he did not happen to know that many women in this country, in speaking of their sex's legs to persons of the other sex, call them distinctively *limbs*, and there drop the subject." Bache also claimed that at a hotel he had heard a women ask her waiter to bring her a trotter, presumably using that not obsolete word rather than *leg*.[28]

Although Marryat's account has long been regarded by some as apocryphal, there is considerable written evidence that this distinction was actually observed in nineteenth-century America. The physician Walter Franklin Robie wrote in 1920 "I must say limb for leg, or some refined lady blushes."[29] And in *The Vinegar Saint,* the poet Hughes Mearns spoke of how "In school one was taught to say limb, and not leg."[30]

The difference between *leg* and *limb* is but one of a number of absurd-seeming distinctions that have been made in English vocabulary. Some of the quibbles of the nineteenth century sound ridiculous to us today, and it is inevitable that some of the words that we today take pains to distinguish will be looked upon humorously in the future.

The notion that one should never use *dilapidated* to refer to a house that was not made of stone (because it comes from the Latin root of *lapis*) was common enough at the beginning of the twentieth century but failed to take hold in influencing the public's use of the word. Richard Grant White thought that the use of *balance* to indicate the remainder of something (as in "the balance of your account") was an "abomination."[31] And Oliver Bell Bunce, the author of the nineteenth-century screed *Don't: A Manual of Mistakes & Improprieties More or Less Prevalent in Conduct and Speech* felt very strongly that *mad* and *angry* were entirely distinct: "Don't use mad for angry" (the reasoning being that *mad* should mean only "insane").[32] These, and many others, are distinctions that have ceased to drive many of us mad.

DONATE

I need hardly say, that this word [*donate*] is utterly abominable—one that any lover of simple honest English cannot hear with patience and without offence.
—Richard Grant White, *Words and Their Uses,* 1872

It is deplorable how far Mr. White is unacquainted with good usage.
—Fitzedward Hall, *Recent Exemplifications of False Philology*, 1872

There were many words that raised the hackles of Richard Grant White. His 1872 work, *Words and Their Uses*, was largely composed of furious attacks on the language use of pretty much anyone else who spoke, wrote, and thought in English. The book, while popular in its day, did not meet with widespread approval from academics—at least not those who studied the English language.

It is tempting to say that Grant reserved special hatred for the word *donate*, except that he appears to have had a similar level of disgust with many other words. Additionally, he was not the only person who had such strong feelings about this word—Oliver Bell Bunce, the author of the aforementioned etiquette book *Don't*, wrote of *donate* and *donation*: "Don't say *donate* when you mean *give*. The use of this pretentious word for every instance of giving has become so common as to be fairly nauseating. . . . If one can not give his church or town library a little money without calling it *donating*, let him, in the name of good English, keep his gift until he has learned better."[33]

Most people today, it seems safe to assume, feel entirely comfortable with using the words *donate* and *donation*. Yet not long ago their use was the subject of widespread condemnation; White and Bunce were not anomalous critics. They shared a similar level of disapproval, if couched in slightly more splenetic language, with many other writers of the early twentieth century. What, you might be wondering, is the problem with these words?

Donate is what we refer to as a back-formation. This is a word that looks as though it were the root of some other, typically longer, form of a word, but which had actually been formed by cutting that longer word down a bit. When we look at words such as *rich* and *richness* we assume (rightly, in this case) that the shorter word came first, and that *richness* was formed by simply adding a suffix to that word. Similarly, we might assume that *donation* came from the earlier form *donate*, except that in this case it did not.

We have a good number of back-formations in English. Some of them are easily recognizable to us, especially if they are of recent origin. Words such as *emote* and *tweeze* seem obviously to be truncated versions of *emotion* and *tweezers*. But we also have words such as *greed*, *televise*, *escalate*, and *aviate*, all of which originated less obviously from longer words (*greedy*, *television*, *escalator*, and *aviation*).

It has been fashionable, for much of the twentieth century, to despise these words. Some of them, such as *enthuse* (a back-formation from *enthusiasm*) have remained verboten in certain circles. Most others, such as *aviate* (from *aviation*) and *automate* (from *automation*), have managed to become assimilated into our language. Before you decide that Richard Grant White was correct in his view of the abomination of *donate*, you should be warned that you would be taking your guidance from a man who also thought that *real estate* was "a mere big-sounding, vulgar phrase for house and land" and "a marked and unjustifiable Americanism," and that *ice cream* was the incorrect form of *iced-cream*.

LIKE

Winston tastes good, like a cigarette should.
—Advertisement for Winston brand cigarettes, 1954

[T]he ad writer who dreamed up the Winston commercial should be jailed.

—Charles Kuralt, in *Harper's Dictionary of Contemporary Usage,* 1975

One evening in the summer of 1954, Walter Cronkite, esteemed and trusted newscaster (popularly known as "the most trusted man in America"), was given a script to read on his nightly broadcast of the news on CBS, much the same as every other night. This one contained text to be read for an advertisement, which was not at all unusual; Cronkite frequently read ads on the air, as did most other newscasters at that time. This particular script, however, contained a four-letter word of Germanic origin, with a *k* in it. Cronkite refused to read it.

That word was *like.*

The promissory slogan containing this offending bit of language has become quite famous, both for its ability to offend lovers of so-called correct English as well as being a superb bit of advertising: "Winston tastes good, *like* a cigarette should." The reluctance that Cronkite felt to speaking these words aloud had nothing to do with the propriety of hawking cigarettes or with the blurred role of newscaster as corporate shill. Rather, it was the use of *like* as a conjunction rather than what was commonly thought of as its appropriate role: as an adverb.

Here we have an extraordinarily clear line of linguistic demarcation. People either feel that using *like* as a conjunction marks one as essentially subliterate or they have absolutely no idea what you are talking about and fail to see why this would be a problem of any sort.

Cronkite, for his part, instead read the words "Winston tastes good, *as* a cigarette should,"[34] inspiring countless armchair pedants in the years since to stick to their insistence on rigid adverbial constructions rather than to accept the semantic broadening of a word that had been assaulting the gates of English in its attempt to be used otherwise for hundreds of years. The mid-twentieth-century American poet Margaret Fishback may have quipped "Whatever its function, like's not a conjunction,"[35] but that would be news to a great number of English-speaking people, who have been using it as one since the 1300s.

Where did this conjunctive *like* come from? No one is certain, but there is widespread speculation that the despised form of the word under discussion was a shortening of *like as*. This presents a puzzle: if *like* and *as* are both shortened forms of *like as*, why is it that *as* has long been considered correct while *like* has been considered a barbarism? This conundrum appears to have not troubled those who have opposed the use of *like*.

The conjunctive *like* began to annoy people in the middle of the eighteenth century, when James Elphinston, in his superbly titled book *The Principles of the English Language Digested*, pointed out that it was antiquated when used in the phrase *like as*. Elphinston used as an example a line from Psalm 103 from the Old Testament: "Like as a father pitieth his own children."[36] By the end of the eighteenth century grammarians were beginning to object to the conjunctive *like* on the grounds that it was incorrect, and not simply outdated. Joseph Hutchins, in *An Abstract of the First Principles of English Grammar*, said that the phrase "He thinks like you do" should instead be written "as you do."[37]

The campaign against *like* continued in the early nineteenth century, picking up steam and disgruntled adherents as it went. It was included in a list of incorrect phrases ("It feels like it has been burned") by Joseph H. Hull in the 1828 book *English Grammar by Lectures*. Shortly after this *like* was condemned by the grammarian and Greek scholar Peter Bullions, who argued that it was an "improper substitution for *as* or *like as*."[38]

As is often the case when a word or usage is thought to be incorrect, the people who used it paid little to no attention to the people who told them that they shouldn't, and *like* was increasingly used as a conjunction throughout the nineteenth century. Much consternation and finger wagging ensued. "The use of 'like' for 'as' is really not considered tolerable in this country by men who have a right to speak on behalf of the English language" wrote an anonymous British writer in 1891,[39] who presumably considered himself to be one of these men. An 1886 review of the novel *Margaret Jermine* noted that "the language is sometimes very bad (witness the use of 'like' for 'as')."[40]

Such "*like* should not be used for *as*" complaints were commonly heard for the ensuing decades, and reached a fevered pitch following the Winston advertisement. The cigarette manufacturer was doubtless delighted by the free publicity they received from the affair, and it is likely that the scorn heaped by the critics served more to convince copywriters to bend the language in hopes of a similar outcome than to scare people away from using *like*.

Winston launched another ad campaign in 1970 in response to the uproar. This ad was a television commercial and featured a professor tediously lecturing students on the error of using *like* as a conjunction. The students suddenly all leap to their feet, wave their packs of cigarettes, and begin to sing "What do you want, good grammar or good taste?" The *Wall Street Journal*, in reporting on this commercial, clucked their tongue and noted "It doesn't matter which you want. In a Winston ad, you don't get either."[41]

The conjunctive form of this word continues to be in wide use today, and condemnation of it has slackened. But now that people have begun to accept *like* as a conjunction (or at least grit their teeth and bear it), new disputed forms have appeared. One must admire this little word, which has proved elastic in its ability to continually shift its use, consistently finding new and original ways to annoy people. *Like* has been negatively associated with "Valley girl" speech (and with the speech of women in general), with the young, with Americans of various locations, and with the uneducated of all kinds.

Writing in the journal *American Speech* in 2007,[42] linguist Alexandra D'Arcy examined many of the myths about the use of this word—including that it is a meaningless word, that only young people use it, and that the "corrupt" use of it is entirely recent. She found none of these assertions to be true: *Like* is used in a wide variety of age groups and countries, most of its uses are not terribly new, and the word always performs some distinct function. Specifically, D'Arcy found that there were four uses of the seemingly meaningless *like* that can be identified: quotative compartmentalizer, approximative adverb, discourse marker, and discourse particle.

Well, that usually ends the conversation.

If one has not had the inestimable pleasure of spending a good deal of time reading through academic linguistic writing, these labels may well sound like the sort of thing someone might come up with in an effort to make fun of how academics write. But they are not nearly as opaque as they first appear, and each one does quite accurately describe a specific way that *like* is used.

Quotative compartmentalizer: "My teacher was *like*, 'You shouldn't say that.'"

Approximative adverb: "It will take me *like* forever to learn these grammar rules."

Discourse marker: "I hate that teacher. *Like*, he was always trying to get us to learn how to spell."

Discourse particle: "And this teacher had *like* totally failed me in that class."

It should be noted that the difference between a discourse marker and a discourse particle is a subtle one, and unless you plan on a career in either studying linguistics or annoying people by informing them of their language habits there is little need to distinguish between them. Discourse markers tend to come at the beginning of sentences or clauses and indicate that an illustration or clarification of what was just said will be given. Particle markers function more as focus markers, and tell the listener that what comes next is of note.

Whether or not you can remember all of these wordy designations for which functions *like* fulfills in conversation (perhaps so that you can nod your head sagely and think to yourself "hmmm . . . nice use of the quotative compartmentalizer" when you ride the subway with a group of linguistically varied teenagers) is not terribly important. It is worthwhile, however, to appreciate that this word *is* fulfilling a function, and it is not a meaningless bit of babble, uttered by your children in an attempt to annoy you. There is very little difference between *like* and *well*, when each is used as a discourse marker, except that *well* is the word that you or your parents sometimes use to begin a sentence ("Well, I didn't *say* you sound stupid when you use *like* as a conjunction"), and *like* is the word that your children, or grandchildren, use.* The fact that a word does not have a readily identifiable meaning does not mean that it serves no purpose.

Another academic who has spent considerable amounts of time puzzling over the use of *like*, Jennifer Dailey-O'Cain, found a startling result when she surveyed people on how they perceived speakers who used this word. Respondents tended to view younger people as less intelligent, but more interesting and friendly, when they used *like* in speech.[43] So take this under advisement if you are under the age of thirty and have long wrestled with the question of whether you would rather be feared or loved.

Some words can't catch a break, no matter how hard they try and will forever be vilified by purists and educators. Such is the fate of *like*. Even the oldest use of the word—active for well over a thousand years—used as a simple verb to denote that . . . well, to say that one *likes* something, has managed to arouse ire in recent years. *Like* has been creeping into the language of social media, in the context of people having the option of clicking a "like" button online after reading an article or viewing a photograph.

Purists have objected that this is not an indication of someone *truly* liking something, much as they have objected to the use of *friend* in similar contexts. Surely these computer-dependent children must be debasing the language by robbing words of their precise meanings, mustn't they? But this seems to be an entirely subjective matter. After all, I find the tastes and mores of teenag-

---

* Etiquette and language guides of the late nineteenth and early twentieth centuries cautioned against using *well* in this fashion, with the objection being similar to the one heard about *like*; that it was meaningless. Ambrose Bierce referred to it as "a mere meaningless prelude to a sentence."

ers (and well-nigh everyone else) to be highly suspect in all regards and so would not feel it is my place to say whether they truly *like* that blog post or not any more than I would question their judgment on electronic music, various types of impractical pants, or varieties of indigestible food.

If you care to adhere to the use of this word in a traditional sense and would like to spend your time excising it with a dull razor from the writings of those who conjunct it, you will at least have a glorious body of literature to spend your time with. For in addition to the copywriters for the Winston cigarette company, the canon of authors who have used *like* as a conjunction contains William Makepeace Thackeray, George Eliot, Emily Brontë, John Keats, and several thousand others whose prose you would otherwise probably enjoy.

six

Defending English

ENGLISH VS. LATIN

There is a common notion that speakers and writers of the English language were far more articulate and composed at some long-ago (and generally undefined) point in the past. The argument usually follows the lines of "the English of several hundred years ago produced Shakespeare and Chaucer; the English of today produces emoticons and Twitter." This conveniently ignores that the literacy rate in the British Isles while Shakespeare was writing these plays was considerably lower than it is today.*

----

* There is some dispute among scholars as to the exact percentage of people who were literate in Elizabethan England, with estimates ranging widely. It is safe to say, however, that literacy among the common population was extremely low.

Whether we are collectively poorer writers now than in Shakespeare's time or not, it is fascinating that one of the longest-running disputes over usage in the English language was current at the time the Bard was writing and continues apace to this day: Why do people insist on using long Latin-based words when they could use short English ones? Is it a matter of trying to sound smarter than one really is, or do these polysyllabic monstrosities actually serve a purpose?

Considering the remarkable impact that the English language has had, spreading like a massive linguistic cancer across the globe, it is puzzling that its defenders seem to have a bit of an inferiority complex about some aspects of its genetic makeup. People have been rushing to defend English vocabulary from the ravening hordes of other languages that have been trying to miscegenate it for about five hundred years. But when we look past the fact that some form of English is today spoken by an estimated one and a half billion people and examine how English was treated in the Middle Ages, it quickly becomes apparent why people in the sixteenth century were so ready to leap to its defense.

After the Norman invasion of 1066 the language of the invaders quickly displaced English in almost all the official writing of the land. Court documents, legal writings, and official proclamations were all written in Norman French. Virtually all scientific writing was in Latin.

The first English translation of the Bible, William Tyndale's version of the New Testament, appeared in 1526. It was not met with universal approval. Hundreds of copies of the book were seized and burned, and several years after its publication Tyndale himself was arrested, put on trial for heresy, and executed by strangulation. Even studies of English were not written in that language. Until the end of the seventeenth century, scholars were still occasionally using Latin to write grammars of the English language.*

William Lambarde, a sixteenth-century antiquarian and legal writer, was the first to come to the defense of English, noting that "our language is fallen *from* the old Inglishe, and drawen nearer to the frenche."[1] Lambarde was doubtless influenced by one of his teachers, a scholar of Old English named Laurence Nowell. Nowell had the courage of his convictions, or something along those lines, for he was so dedicated to preserving English that he appears to have invented a number of words for his collection of Old English vocabulary, just so people would not have to stoop to using Latin.[2]

Shortly after Lambarde's peevish comment appeared, the defense of English began to be seen in other published writings. A man named Sir John Cheke translated the Gospels of Matthew and Mark into English and substituted Anglo-Saxon terms such as *hundreder* for *centurion, ill-speed* for *blasphemy,* and *gainrising* for *resurrection.* Cheke was a noted classical scholar of the sixteenth century—he taught Greek at Cambridge, tutored Prince Edward, and held the position of "gentleman of the privy" (which, rather than indicating that he was a washroom attendant, indicates that he was a trusted adviser to the king). An oft-quoted line of Cheke's is "I am of this opinion that our tung should be written cleane and pure, vnmixt and vnmangled with borrowing of other tunges."[3]

Cheke, along with other rhetoricians of his time, waged war on the infusion of Greek and Latin words that were then being

---

* The last such book was Christopher Cooper's *Grammatica Linguæ Anglicanæ,* published in 1685.

imported into English. Often these words were the creation of writers who obviously wanted to embellish their prose with a fine-looking specimen and so would grab a long classical word, stick an Anglicized ending on it, and throw it onto the page, hoping for the best. Although widely derided as ridiculous affectations by some, the creators of these words were well intentioned: They sought to elevate English to the level of other, presumably nobler, languages, and thought that adding fancy words would help.

The sixteenth-century logician Ralph Lever thought so little of words of Latinate origin that he made a point of avoiding them in the title of his *Art of Reason, Rightly Termed Witcraft* (the word *reason* came into English through the French *raison*, which in turn was from the Latin root of *ration-*). In this book Lever came up with a number of Saxon-derived new words (what he referred to as "native" terms) to replace those of Latin origin. Unfortunately for him, he found that most people did not understand them and so had to add a glossary to the end of the book, explaining what they meant.[4] In a section titled "A Note to Vnderstand the Meaning of New Deuised Termes" Lever offers up *saywhat* (for *definition*), *endsay* (for *conclusion*), and *wight* (for *animal*).

These Latinate words that so inflamed Cheke and Lever were referred to as *inkhorns*, and they are part of one of the more ridiculous chapters in the history of English. Many people hated them and thought of them as buffoonish attempts to make a writer appear more elegant. Few people hated them more than the author of a delightfully splenetic little pamphlet titled "*Vindex Anglicus*," published in 1644. The small work was written by an anonymous writer and had the subtitle "The Perfections of the English Language Defended, and Asserted." It contained a title page, approximately six pages of text, and the author appeared to be quite unaware of the irony in attaching a Latin phrase (*Vin-*

dex Anglicus translates to "defender of English") to a screed on the necessity of avoiding Latin-based vocabulary.

Vindex begins by defending English reasonably enough, making note of some of the more useful features of our language (that it is rich in synonyms, abounds in graceful expressions, and many of our words have multiple shades of meaning). Soon after the author warms to his task by enumerating some of the flaws that may be found in other languages: Italian is "an excellent, princely, and pleasant Language . . . yet it wants Sinews" and has too many vowels, French is "too affected and delicate," Spanish is "terrible and boisterous," while Dutch is "manly, but very harsh" and has too many consonants.[5]

Having loosened himself up by offering these opinions of the continental tongues, the pamphleteer then feels limber enough to unleash full fury on those fools who insist on debasing English through the use of what we today would refer to as two-dollar words. Stating that he will offer the reader some examples of these words, the author prefaces this list with the admonition: "read and censure."

One must admit that many of the words that the author of *Vindex* found objectionable do seem rather overwrought, if amusing. There are words such as *bulbitate* (poetically defined in the *OED* as "to befilth one's breech"),* *lurcate* ("to eat in a ravenous manner"), and *ligurition* ("greediness").

Yet even if these words seem absurd to us today, they really are not much different from many words that we use without a second thought. Most of us are untroubled by *equivocate, compassionate,* and *inoculate*; these are all words that have been formed the same

----

* Another way of saying "defecate in one's pants."

way as the inkhorns were, through the Anglicizing of a Latin word. They just have the benefit of having had their edges smoothed down through familiarity.

For the most part these kinds of fanciful words of the sixteenth and seventeenth centuries died a quick and natural death, living on only in books of the time, and historical records of the language, such as the *Oxford English Dictionary*. The author of *Vindex* appears to have been largely correct when he stated, "Our language is copious enough already," believing that these words would not last.

But he was not entirely correct—several of the words he thought were unnecessary and ridiculous coinages ended up working their way into the English language. *Contrast*, for example, is a word that few people today would think of as fantastical, yet it is one of the words condemned in *Vindex*, as is *mephitic*.* Picking which words will last and which will not, in any language, is an extremely difficult thing to do.

This difficulty has not stopped many from trying, however. A particularly common way of doing this has been to affirm the need of preserving "pure" English vocabulary, rather than employing words of Latin origins. One of the problems with attempting to enforce any sort of pure English is the fact that so much of our vocabulary does not come from English roots. The word *pure*, for instance, is itself taken from Latin (*purus*). If we wanted to keep such a phrase entirely within the realm of our presumed linguistic heritage we would have to use the Old English *clæne* (since that

---

* *Mephitic*, meaning "offensive smelling," is not a terribly common word, but it has survived into present-day English, with citations from a wide variety of technical and literary authors.

was their word for *pure*), and "clǽne English" just doesn't sound right. Cheke's "opinion that our tung should be written cleane and pure, vnmixt and vnmangled with borrowing of other tunges" serves as another example of the difficulty in keeping English undefiled, as his statement contains three words that are of Latin, rather than Old English, origin (*opinion, unmixt,* and *pure*).[*]

Putting aside the myriad modern contaminants that have enriched our tongue, the English language has long been a hodgepodge, born of invasion and strife. What we think of as modern English comes from Middle English, which was heavily influenced by the French, after they invaded the British Isles in 1066. What about before that, was the language used in the British Isles pure English? Not quite. It was Old English, the language that is responsible for much of our current grammatical structure as well as much of our core vocabulary.[†]

But Old English is not quite the Ur-English that some would like it to be. After all, Old English is also commonly known as Anglo-Saxon, so called after the Angles and Saxons, who invaded England (along with the Jutes) in the fifth century. These three groups come from what would more or less translate in modern geographic terms as Germany and Denmark. When these invaders arrived they displaced the languages that had been spoken, which were several forms of Celtic. Old English itself is the lan-

----

[*] Although in defense of Cheke, he never advocated getting rid of Latinate words that were already established in English; he just wanted new words to be drawn from an Anglo-Saxon well.

[†] The vocabulary of English is currently 70 to 80 percent composed of words of Greek and Latin origin, but it is certainly not a Romance language, it is a Germanic one. Evidence of this may be found in the fact that it is quite easy to create a sentence without words of Latin origin, but pretty much impossible to make one that has no words from Old English.

guage of an invader. And not just an invader, but one that was remarkably successful in stamping out the languages it displaced, for there is extremely little evidence of the Celtic languages that were spoken before Angles and Saxons arrived.

"But surely," say some (and by "some" I mean those who wish to bring back the highly inflected language of a thousand years back) "surely Old English was, for all intents and purposes, the first *real* language introduced to England" (once we killed most of the Celts, that is). It is close to being first, and is predated by only four hundred years by Latin.

Before the Angles and Saxons, the region had also been host to a Roman invasion, occurring in about 43 BCE, which had provided some Latin influence on the vocabulary. Words such as *butyrum* (which became *butter*), *mulus* (which became *mule*), and *balteus* (which became *belt*) are all Latin words that were used in England before Anglo-Saxon and which have worked their way into our language today. As mentioned, Latin was spoken in England before English was, about four centuries earlier.

Latin influences on English can be categorized into four different waves. The first was through the original Roman conquest. This initial contact with Latin left few words. Following this, additional Latin words were introduced through Christian missionaries who traveled to Britain. The third wave, and largest to date, occurred through the Norman French of the eleventh-century invaders, which was itself largely derived from Latin. And the final wave came from the invented scientific vocabulary of the following centuries.

However, the fact that pure English is itself neither etymologically nor historically pure has been entirely overlooked, as many people over the years have spent considerable time and effort in the pursuit of keeping English pure by pushing Latin out of it. The anti-inkhorn crowd of the sixteenth and seventeenth centuries passed their baton to subsequent writers, and there have ever since been people who are interested in promoting the mythical Englishness of English.

In the eighteenth century Noah Webster wrote, "We see continually a wretched jargon of Latin and English in every merchant's book, even to the exclusion of a pure English phrase, more concise, more correct, and more elegant."[6] And George Campbell, in *The Philosophy of Rhetoric*, wrote that "our language is in greater danger of being overwhelmed by an inundation of foreign words, than of any other species of destruction."[7]

The next century saw Herbert Spencer's *Philosophy of Style*, which argued that a Saxon vocabulary provided a "greater forcibleness" and was preferable to a Latinate one. He based this on the fact that children tend to learn the Saxon words before they learn the polysyllabic ones as well as the fact that Saxon words were shorter. Winston Churchill is often quoted in an approving fashion by people who like their words short and Saxon: "Short words are best and the old words when short are best of all."[8] Like so many Churchill sayings, the version that is commonly quoted is not quite the entire quote; he began the sentence with the words "Broadly speaking," which makes it less of a declarative ultimatum and more of a personal preference.

This desire to excise Roman influence from one's vocabulary continued strongly in the twentieth century. *The King's English*, written by the Fowler brothers in 1906, told readers that they should "prefer the Saxon word to the Romance."[9] E. B. White, in *Elements of Style*, cautioned that "Anglo-Saxon is a livelier tongue than Latin, so use Anglo-Saxon words." Proponents of what is sometimes referred to as Saxonism have typically been picky about what aspects of this language they want to rescue: Many have sought to retain the short words found in it, but few have advocated a resurrection of the enormously complex system of inflections that governed the language.

There was one document in the twentieth century that was particularly associated, whether rightly or wrongly, with the notion that it is preferable to use English-origin words rather than Latinate ones: George Orwell's "Politics and the English Language."

Published in 1946 in the journal *Horizon*, Orwell's polemic against unwieldy prose has provided fodder both for those who feel, as Orwell did, that "the English language is in a bad way" as well as those who feel that it was Orwell himself who was in a bad way. Proponents of Orwell's view hold that he was issuing a much needed call for clarity in writing; opponents have pointed out that many of his suggestions are impractical, so much so that Orwell often does not follow them himself.

It does seem pertinent to note that Orwell was attempting to address, as the title of his essay makes clear, the subject of *politics* in writing English—he makes no arguments that his suggestions should be followed when writing poetry ("I have not here been considering the literary use of language"). But Orwell does not really confine himself to talking about political language, and since the nicety of his essay's title is often ignored by both those in favor of Orwell and those against him, it is worth examining his views on this matter. They represent much that is problematic with how we think about "correct" use of language and to whom we look to provide us with guidance on this matter.

Orwell was certainly a fine writer, at least in the estimation of a considerable portion of the English-speaking world, and there is no doubt that he was an influential one. His novels and essays have proved to have had remarkable longevity, and there are few who would say that he is not one of the major figures of English letters in the last century. But is he an authority on language? He has offered himself as one, and so it is worth examining whether this position is well founded.

The easiest (and sometimes the most unfair) way of judging someone who is in the position of arbiter on language is to apply their rules and suggestions to their own writing, to see how they stack up. Grammarians have been doing this to each other, in vicious fashion, for hundreds of years, and it always provides amusement, for there are very few writers who always follow their own advice. Orwell is exceptional in this regard only in that he breaks his own rules far more frequently than most language scolds do, often disregarding his advice in the very same sentence in which he offers it.

In "Politics and the English Language," Orwell offers six rules, which he proposes "will cover most cases," and here they are, in order, followed by an examination of whether he follows them himself. To be fair to Orwell, we will judge him based primarily on whether he follows these rules in the same essay in which he proposed them.

1. "Never use a metaphor, simile, or other figure of speech which you are used to seeing in print." To say that this rule is not observed in Orwell's writing is a dramatic understatement. In fact, he breaks the rule so egregiously that readers must wonder if he understands what a metaphor is. Earlier in the essay he cautions against using metaphors . . . by using a metaphor: "There is a long list of *flyblown* metaphors which could similarly be got rid of." Unless these metaphors that Orwell dislikes were actually infested with the larvae of some species of fly, it is obvious that he is using the word *flyblown* in a metaphoric sense. Furthermore, whether or not it is a lovely or useful metaphor, it is a long-established one, having been in figurative use in English continuously since 1528, when John Skelton wrote of responding to the "flyblowen opynions"[10] of others, and so Orwell must have seen it previously in print.

In the second sentence of his essay Orwell writes of the potential "collapse" of both our language and civilization, even though neither one of these things can actually collapse except in a metaphorical sense. "Politics and the English Language" is likewise liberally sprinkled with similes ("like cavalry horses answering the bugle," "A mass of Latin words falls upon the facts like soft snow," "like a cuttlefish spurting out ink"), none of which is original to Orwell.

2. "Never use a long word where a short one will do." "Politics and the English Language," unfortunately enough for those who do not care for long words, has no shortage of these polysyllabic creatures. And one can almost always find a short word to replace them with. Orwell writes "A speaker who uses that kind of phraseology has gone some distance toward turning himself into a machine," a sentence in which *phraseology* could be replaced by *language* or *words*. Later he writes that it should be possible "to make pretentiousness unfashionable." He could certainly have used *pretension* instead of *pretentiousness*, as it has a similar meaning and would have saved him five letters. So why didn't he? Perhaps he just liked the way *pretentiousness* looked on the page, which is a fine reason to put it there. In another example of the sort of long word that Orwell dislikes, he mentions writers who fall into the habit of using the *de-* and *-ize* formations with their verbs. Yet he himself has no trouble with writing "it is natural to fall into a pretentious, *Latinized* style" in this essay.

3. "If it is possible to cut a word out, always cut it out." It would be rather petty to go through this essay to find a list of words that may be cut out, but when confronted with needlessly restrictive rules for language use I become a petty sort of fellow. So I will offer the following examples, with the words that could be cut out underlined:

> "It is <u>rather</u> the same thing that is happening to the English language."
> "<u>Yet without a doubt</u> it is the second kind of sentence that is gaining ground in modern English."
> "If it is possible to cut a word <u>out</u>, always cut it <u>out</u>."

4. "Never use the passive voice where you can use the active." In the very first sentence of his essay Orwell tells us that "Most people who bother with the matter at all would admit that the English language is in a bad way," and after pausing to insert a comma to catch his breath, informs us that "*it is generally assumed* that we cannot by conscious action do anything about it" (italics mine). Orwell's sentence, needless to say, features a passive construction, and one that could have been avoided by writing either "people generally assume," "we all generally assume," or some such other noble active voicing. Orwell uses the passive voice quite often throughout this essay, and in every case he could have found a way to use the active. For example, in referring to the type of writing he abhors, Orwell notes that "the passive voice is wherever possible used in preference to the active," a sentence that is itself a fine example of using the passive. The reason to not use the active in every single case is that sometimes it just sounds awful.

The *Merriam-Webster Dictionary of English Usage*, in a finely tuned rebuttal to Orwell's dictum on the passive voice, notes that he uses it quite a bit more than most writers do, and adds "Clearly he found the construction useful in spite of his advice to avoid it as much as possible." In her 1962 book *Current American Usage*, Margaret Bryant found that the passive voice was used in general expository writing approximately 10 percent of the time; the aforementioned entry found in *Webster* points out that in his essay Orwell employs it slightly more than twice as often.

5. "Never use a foreign phrase, a scientific word, or a jargon word if you can think of an everyday English equivalent." Orwell does in fact follow this advice in this particular essay, and we should commend him for it. It is the only one of his rules that he does not violate in the same breath that he formulated it. However, he was not so opposed to using these items in other writing. He helpfully provides a list of phrases to avoid ("Foreign words and expressions such as *cul de sac, ancien regime, deus ex machina, mutatis mutandis, status quo, gleichschaltung, weltanschauung* are used to give an air of culture and elegance."), several of which he uses regularly in other essays and books. In *Homage to Catalonia*, Orwell writes of people resisting Franco "in the name of 'democracy' and the *status quo*," and in his essay on Charles Dickens he writes "the *deus ex machina* enters with a bag of gold in the last chapter and the hero is absolved from further struggle."

6. "Break any of these rules sooner than say anything outright barbarous." This is the one rule that Orwell scrupulously adheres to and employs with gusto. The examples given earlier represent a small number of the times that he violates his rules, although I will leave it to more discerning literary types to decide whether he has avoided saying anything barbarous.

But given that Orwell breaks every one of his own rules except for the one that allows him to break his rules, it is somewhat questionable why so many people should view this essay approvingly as a *vade mecum* for English usage. The fact that he so often violates these rules in the same sentence that he pronounces them makes it even more questionable, as if we were influenced by a grammar book that informed us "sentences always end with a period" and then failed to include any such punctuation marks.

Having worked through this screed against Orwell's feelings on the passive and unnecessary words, let us turn again to what he has to say on the subject of using pure English. According to Orwell, "Bad writers, and especially scientific, political, and sociological writers, are nearly always haunted by the notion that Latin or Greek words are grander than Saxon ones and unnecessary words like *expedite, ameliorate, predict, extraneous, deracinated, clandestine, subaqueous,* and hundreds of others constantly gain ground from their Anglo-Saxon numbers." While there is certainly a case to be made against bad writers using pompous words, it is not at all clear that the words listed by Orwell have supplanted Anglo-Saxon ones; for instance, there is no word for *expedite* in Old English.

Orwell also thought that "it should be possible . . . to reduce the amount of Latin and Greek in the average sentence." It is difficult to view Orwell as an accurate prognosticator on this point as it comes shortly after he has just made the claim that "silly words and expressions have often disappeared . . . owing to the conscious action of a minority," claiming that "the jeers of a few journalists" have done away with the phrases *explore every avenue* and *leave no stone unturned.* Orwell and other journalists may well have scoffed at these shopworn phrases, but this scorn did nothing to curtail their use. *Leave no stone unturned* continued to be in widespread use after Orwell's report of its demise, and *explore every avenue* appears to have increased in frequency in the several decades after the publication of "Politics and the English Language."*

But the idea that there must be a way to get all the right-thinking people together to do something about the abuse of English, whether through the jeers of journalists or through the creation of an institution is not unique to Orwell. It is an idea that has almost five hundred years of failure under its belt.

AN ENGLISH ACADEMY

English is the official language of England, unsurprisingly enough (although it was French for several hundred years). The United States, to the chagrin of many who would have it otherwise, has no official language. And there has never been an official governing body for the English language. For many people who think that English requires nightly baths and strict supervision, this is the linguistic equivalent of raising a child on a steady diet of potato chips and cupcakes, giving them no curfew, and always telling them that they are special, no matter what.

Many countries have enacted national standards to govern their language, or to at least make an attempt at doing so. French has L'Académie française, which for almost four hundred years has struggled to bring a sense of order to the French language.

----

* While this is not a scientific study, a look at the newspapers contained in Access Newspaper Archive (newspaperarchive.com) indicates that this phrase increased in the decades after Orwell's pronouncement of death. It was used 88 times in the 1940s, 236 times in the 1950s, and 614 times in the 1960s.

Italian has the Academia della Crusca,* which fulfills a similar role.

In some cases an academy has been formed to preserve what is feared to be a dying language, while in other cases it seems to be simply that they don't want another language to intrude on their personal space. This can occasionally lead to awkward contortions, as when the French Academy announced that they would ban the English imports *le cash-box* (despite the fact that *cash* comes from the French word *casse*), and *label* (which comes from the French word *label*, meaning ribbon).

There have been repeated calls to create a regulating body that would guard English against the pernicious efforts of foreigners, poets, and teenagers, all of whom seek to render it impure. In 1752, George Harris, writing in *Observations upon the English Language*, sounded almost wistful as he thought of the possibilities afforded by creating such an academy:

> Sometimes I imagine that a Grammar and Dictionary,
> published under the Inspection of an Academy, would
> not sufficiently ascertain our Language without the
> Assistence of the Legislature: but lest you should think
> that I would indeavour to force men by Law to write
> with Propriety and Correctness of Style, I must de-
> clare, that I mean only to force them to spell with
> Uniformity according to certain given patterns, and
> without Elisions: and I am not only confident, that
> such a Uniformity in Spelling might easily be effected,

----

* The name translates to "academy of the bran," supposedly because their mission was to separate the figurative bran of the language from its flour.

but that it would alone be sufficient to preserve our
Language intire to the most distant Times; and I can
not but esteem the English Language to be of such
Consequence to Englishmen in general, that a proper
Act, for the Improvement and Preservation of it,
would do Honor to an English Parliament.[11]

The fact that no fewer than four of the words in Harris's screed
(*assistence, indeavour, intire*, and *can not*) are spelled in a markedly
different fashion from the way we would spell them today serves,
depending on one's perspective, as either a cautionary tale for the
need to have such an academy or the foolhardiness of trying to
create one.

Harris was not the first to propose such legislation. The earliest mention of such an idea appears to be found in a letter from
the writer Gabriel Harvey to the poet Edmund Spenser in 1580.
Harvey was concerned mainly with poetry, and the spelling of
English words, and, although he wished to see "an acte of Parliament," he apparently did not pursue the matter.[12]

The first actual attempt to create a legislative body for this
purpose came in 1617, when Edmund Bolton* tried to create an
English academy (what he at the time called an "academ roial"),
one that would be devoted to such topics as heraldry, history, and
the English language. Despite having some support at court,

----

* The *Oxford Dictionary of National Biography* refers to Bolton as "an important English
antiquary of the second rank" and notes that "His various writings, and his largely
unsuccessful career, reveal Bolton to have been a man of great ambition but scant
financial means, who pressed his causes on his friends and prospective patrons with
a persistence that sometimes caused ill will."

Bolton's scheme went nowhere, and the would-be protector of our language died penniless a decade or so later.

But after the successful creation of the French Academy in 1635, attempts to similarly preserve English began once again. There were numerous attempts to create an official body that would reform, preserve, or otherwise guard the language. Jonathan Swift and Daniel Defoe were two of the many luminaries of English literature who sought to bring about such an academy. Their efforts, and those of all who followed them, came to naught.

One of the themes often heard in the call for the preservation of English was the need for a respectable dictionary. In the middle of the eighteenth century there appeared a magnificent one, and the hope arose that it could be used to "fix" the language. This dictionary was Samuel Johnson's 1755 *Dictionary of the English Language*.

Of people who have been in a position to effect a profound influence on the English language, few rank above Johnson, whose dictionary is rightfully regarded as one of the greatest lexicographic works ever composed, and all the more so as it was largely the work of a single man. There has likely been more written about Johnson's dictionary than any other such book, and it would be tiresome to provide a drawn-out explanation of why it was special. Johnson's dictionary was not particularly innovative—he was not the first, as is commonly supposed, to write an English dictionary, nor was he the first in adding to his dictionary any of the things that we associate with dictionaries. Previous lexicographers had made attempts to catalog all the words in English, had included etymologies of words, pronunciations, illustrative citations, and usage notes. What Johnson did was improve on the work of his predecessors.

One of the most interesting aspects of Johnson's dictionary, his desire to fix the language, doesn't even come up in that book; it is found in his plan for the dictionary, published eight years earlier. Johnson, like many writers and scholars of the time, largely depended on the support of a patron, in this case Philip Dormer, Earl of Chesterfield, who had provided Johnson with funds to aid in his endeavors.* The plan for the dictionary was a combination of fawning dedication to the man who would aid him financially in creating it as well as a description of what that work would contain.

Johnson's plan carefully explained how he would arrange his dictionary and the hopes he had for it. Addressing Chesterfield directly, he wrote: "This, my Lord, is my idea of an English dictionary; a dictionary by which the pronunciation of our language may be fixed, and its attainment facilitated; by which its purity may be preserved, its use ascertained, and its duration lengthened."[13] Somewhat earlier in the plan Johnson asserted that "Barbarous, or impure, words and expressions, may be branded with some note of infamy, as they are carefully to be eradicated wherever they are found." Johnsonian scholars have varied in their opinion of how much of this Johnson believed. Some hold that he was overplaying his prescriptivist tendencies to please his patron (who was well known for his desire to rid English of impurities), as Johnson does mention in his plan that language change is inevitable. Others, however, feel that the avowal to fix the language did indeed represent Johnson's view at that time.

----

* The relationship between Johnson and Chesterfield came to an unhappy end, after the earl declined to continue providing money, leading to one of the most frequently quoted definitions in Johnson's book: *Patron*: "Commonly a wretch who supports with insolence, and is paid with flattery."

Eight years is a remarkably short time in which to write an entire dictionary, especially one written by a single man (the first edition of the *Oxford English Dictionary* was published, in installments, over the course of forty-four years and was the work of hundreds of compilers), but it is a long time to sit in a room staring at words. And over the course of these eight years, Johnson's views on fixing the language, at least those he had outlined in his plan, changed considerably.

By the time the dictionary was finished, Johnson's opinions on language change bore little resemblance to the ones he espoused in his plan. One of the ways this was most in evidence was in how he described the notion of an academy of English: "If an academy should be established for the cultivation of our stile, which I . . . hope the spirit of English liberty will hinder or destroy, let them, instead of compiling grammars and dictionaries, endeavour, with all their influence, to stop the licence of translatours."[14] By the late 1770s, when Johnson wrote his *Lives of Poets*, his opinion on an academy was even more pronounced: "In this country an academy could be expected to do but little. . . . The edicts of an English academy would, probably, be read by many, only that they might be sure to disobey them."[15]

Attempts to fix the English language have not been restricted to the British. In the 1780s a group of Americans, led in large part by John Adams, proposed creating an institution for "refining, improving, and ascertaining the English language."[16] They were soon joined by Noah Webster, who wrote, "I am fully of the opinion, that the reformation of the language we speak, will some time or other be thought an object of legislative importance."[17]

But Adams's plan went nowhere, and Webster followed a path

similar to that of Samuel Johnson. Several decades after having written about the legislative importance of regulating the language, he too decided that the idea was flawed: "I think it would be unfortunate that any state or distinct section of our great republic should determine absolutely upon a standard of speaking or writing the common language of [the] American nation."[18]

Calls for an American academy of English continued, with no actually legislative bodies ever being created, through to the twentieth century. This is not to say that there have been no attempts to regulate or change the language by fiat. There have been, but they failed miserably.

On August 24, 1906, Theodore Roosevelt used the power of the office of the presidency to indulge in one of his pet peeves about the English language: its confusing spelling. Roosevelt issued an executive decree, informing the government printing office that henceforth three hundred words would no longer be spelled the way they had been. Such words as *kissed* would become *kist*, *looked* would be *lookt*, and *surprise* would become *surprize*.

The idea was widely mocked in newspapers, and the government printers did not act on Roosevelt's ruling. Congress later voted overwhelmingly in favor of overturning the order.

Today there are few serious attempts to create an authoritative body to govern our language. The calls for preserving the sanctity of proper English are more often found in independent organizations with no legislative agenda, such as the Queen's English Society, whose website says "we refuse as a nation to adopt the word 'sidewalk' when there is already a perfectly good word—pavement—nicely settled in our language."[19]

The Queen's English Society maintains that our language is

in a continuing state of deterioration and feels strongly that efforts to stop this decline are in order: "There are always going to be slips in live broadcasting, but writers, programme makers and the people who appear on TV and radio, or write for our newspapers must, if necessary, be embarrassed into striving for the highest possible standards in the use of English."[20]

The notion that embarrassment will serve as linguistic curative is certainly preferable to advocating beating people for failing to adhere to rules. But we have been embarrassing people for language mistakes for hundreds of years now, and still these mistakes occur. Are we perhaps not embarrassing them enough or is this method of instruction a flawed one?

Time and again we hear the refrain: If we fail to diligently observe the distinction between certain words we will lose something beautiful and irreplaceable in our tongue; our language is being mutilated and debased and requires constant vigilance to guard against the reprobates who would do it harm. Is there any evidence that a lack of such care will lead to such a state?

Let's once again look back to English at the time of the Norman invasion. When these Gallic interlopers arrived on the shores of England, the language they displaced was Old English. For more than a hundred years this forbear of the English language was displaced in schools, government, and writing. Few people paid any attention to how it fared, let alone actively guarded against depredations that might weaken it. No one was correcting the speech or writing of children, there were no guides to promote the proper use of *hopefully*, and by and large the language was left to fend for itself. What was the result? We ended up with Middle English, the language of Geoffrey Chaucer and Sir Thomas Malory.

SHAKESPEARE'S LANGUAGE

The name William Shakespeare will immediately spring to the mind of many people when asked who is the greatest writer in the English language. This is true even if they don't think so, simply because there is an expectation that so many other people do (Tolstoy was a notable exception—he despised the Bard's work). Without seeking to diminish Shakespeare's importance in our canon, it is worth examining some of the ways that we think about the Bard and language, in particular the notion of Shakespeare as linguistic inventor.

For much of the twentieth century there have been two beliefs about Shakespeare and his use of English that were unquestioned: He had a massive vocabulary and he invented a very large portion of the words he used. Both of these statements are true, but not quite in the way that we often think.

The notion that Shakespeare had an unusually large vocabulary is based on a count of all the words he used in his writing; it is somewhere between fifteen and thirty thousand. We know he used all these words because there have been people who were extremely passionate about Shakespeare for hundreds of years now, and some of them went through his work in the nineteenth century and made concordances, in which they listed every word he ever used in his writings, cataloging where they were used in his plays and poetry. This was considerably more difficult before the Internet made this a trick you can do on your phone. The fact that even with someone who has been so exhaustively studied as Shakespeare there remains a range of about fifteen thousand words in estimates of his vocabulary size indicates how difficult it can be to make such conclusions.

However, assuming that Shakespeare knew about twenty thousand words or word forms (the figure agreed upon by most scholars), does this constitute having a large vocabulary? It is difficult to say since there is very little agreement about how many words anyone knows. On the one hand this seems like a simple matter to clear up: You either know a word or you don't, and if you know it you make a little check next to that word and go on to the next one. But once you begin to think about it, it quickly becomes apparent that accurately measuring numbers of words in this fashion is quite difficult.

Suppose you ask me if I know the word *run*, and I reply in the affirmative—do we say that I know one word? Suppose I explain that I know that *run* can be a point scored in a baseball game, a jog in a park, a tear in a stocking, and a string of winning games of any kind—do we still say that I know one word, or do I know four? If I know what *run*, *ran*, and *running* all mean—is that three words or one? *Run* represents what we call a lexeme (what you might think of as a headword in a dictionary), and *ran* and *running* are forms of this lexeme.

And this is to say nothing of what it means to actually *know* a word—does it mean that, as Potter Stewart said about obscenity, that one knows it when one sees it? Or must one be able to define a word in order to say that one knows it? Because of such vagaries, we have seen an exceedingly wide range in the estimated vocabulary sizes of English-speaking people. Some academics have placed the vocabulary size of an average high school graduate at 5,000,[21] while others have said that it is closer to 17,000,[22] or 45,000.[23] At the upper end of the scale, a pair of researchers in 1940 estimated that the number of words that some adults may know is 150,000,[24] and other researchers still have suggested that the number might be as high as 250,000.[25] There is, needless to say, a rather large gap between knowing 5,000 and 250,000 words, and yet both these figures are often bandied about as being representative of the size of our vocabulary.

But once again, we are assuming, for the sake of argument and brevity, that Shakespeare was familiar with twenty thousand words and that this meant that he was considerably wordier than your average Elizabethan. Where did we get the idea that he had invented 10 percent of his words?

When the *Oxford English Dictionary* was finished in 1928 it was the first completed attempt to provide a historical record of English use. This dictionary provided two and a half million citations of words in use, as a means of illustrating how the words in the dictionary behaved in real life. One of the main goals of the dictionary was to provide the earliest use of a new word or new sense of that word. Each sense of a word had chronologically arranged citations, so it was quite easy to see which author had provided the first citation for some particular use of a word.

So when the public got their hands on this historical treasure it was only natural that someone would go through the dictionary to see how many entries listed Shakespeare as the first one to use a word. It was an astonishingly high number—slightly more than two thousand lexemes. This dwarfed the number of first citations for any other writer except Chaucer.* Since many concordances of Shakespeare's work give a word (or lexeme) count of twenty thousand, the math seemed pretty simple—20,000 ÷ 2,000 = 10

---

* Charlotte Brewer has pointed out that Chaucer's numbers are due to the fact that his works were so much more readily available than those of any other medieval writer at the time that the dictionary was first compiled.

percent, therefore Shakespeare invented 10 percent of the words that he used.

This reasoning assumes that the *Oxford English Dictionary* would not have missed any authors using these words before Shakespeare did, which is not the case. The *OED* has never claimed that the first examples of words they provide are absolutely the first time the word has ever been used, merely that they represent the earliest evidence that the editors of the dictionary have been able to find. Much of this evidence was found by volunteer readers who would send slips of paper with citations written on them to the *OED*, and these readers really liked to read Shakespeare.

So many of these volunteer readers wanted to review Shakespeare that it resulted in a fairly severe overrepresentation of his work in the dictionary. In addition to the two thousand quotes in the *OED* containing words that Shakespeare ostensibly used for the first time there were another thirty-one thousand citations of the Bard's—a total of thirty-three thousand citations. The second most quoted author was Walter Scott, who, while certainly amply cited, has fewer than half as many citations as Shakespeare (about fifteen thousand).

The problem here is not that the *OED* had tens of thousands of citations from Shakespeare (there is nothing factually inaccurate about that) or even that the *OED* had two thousand words for which Shakespeare provided the first citation: These words were credited to Shakespeare based on the information that the editors of the *OED* had available to them. The problem is that people then assumed that he must have made up all of these words, and that was not the case.

There are many instances in which a word long thought to

have been invented by Shakespeare was used previously by some lesser-known writer. For instance, Shakespeare is currently listed in the *OED* as the first author to use the word *ceremoniously*, in *The Merchant of Venice* (1600): "Ceremoniously let vs prepare some welcome for the Mistres of the house." However, the word had been used at least as far back as 1574, when Arthur Golding used it in a translation of Jean Calvin: "very ceremoniously pretende that God shall be honored."[26]

Similarly, Shakespeare has long been thought to have coined the word *hunchbacked*, using it in Richard III, in one of his more memorable string of insults: "That bottled spider, that foule bunch-backt toade." Again, the word was in use before this, as we find it, with the same variant spelling, in Thomas Hill's 1571 work, *The Contemplation of Mankind*: "as are the bunch backed, and gogle eyed persons."[27] Neither of these two words has been edited recently in the *OED*, and when they are it is certain that the dictionary will find and record these earlier uses.

The *OED* began revising the third edition of the dictionary in 2000, a rather large effort that entails reediting every one of hundreds of thousands of entries. It is an endeavor that will take several decades to finish. This work-in-progress is being updated online in a digitally searchable format and so allows researchers the opportunity to see how many of the words that were long thought to have been coined by Shakespeare were in fact used before him.

In a paper published in *Shakespeare Survey* in 2013, Charlotte Brewer compared the number of entries listing Shakespeare as the first citation in various editions of the *OED*. Comparing all such entries that occurred in the entry range from letter *M* to the word *rotness* (which was what had been recently edited by that point), she found that approximately 30 percent of the words that were previously thought to have been coined by Shakespeare were now recorded in the *OED* as having an earlier author. Additionally, she discovered that the rate at which Shakespeare was being ante-dated in the third edition of the *OED* was growing, as an increasing number of online databases composed of fifteenth- and sixteenth-century writers became available to the editors of the dictionary.[28] At the time of this writing, Shakespeare is listed in the *OED* as being the first author to use about sixteen hundred words, as opposed to the more than two thousand he was originally credited with. This is still an impressive number, although it is certain to continue to diminish as the editors of the *OED* continue their revisions.

Several other academics have recently analyzed the size of Shakespeare's vocabulary in order to assess whether his word hoard was as much larger than his contemporaries as has long been thought. In a paper published in *Shakespeare Quarterly* in 2011, the computational linguist Hugh Craig compared Shakespeare's vocabulary to that of his peers, late-sixteenth- and early-seventeenth-century playwrights. Craig found that Shakespeare did indeed use more words than most of his contemporaries, with about 20,000 distinct words in his plays (Ben Jonson used almost as many, about 18,500).[29] However, he was writing about a much wider range of subjects than the other playwrights, which somewhat explains why he used more words. Additionally, he has more surviving works than other playwrights of that time, because, well, because he was Shakespeare, and even back then people knew this writing was special. Of course, the genius of Shakespeare's writing lies not in the quantity of words he used, but in the way he put them together.

In a similar vein, David Crystal points out in his book *Think on My Words* that most present-day writers have a vocabulary that exceeds Shakespeare's.[30] This is not due to any accomplishment on our part, but simply because the English language is considerably larger today than it was four hundred years ago, and we have all been exposed to a far broader range of language.

However, as Brewer also points out, a new feature of the *OED*'s website allows users of the dictionary to search not only for the first author to use a word but also the first to use a word in a specific sense. When viewing Shakespeare in this light, not only as a linguistic inventor who created words but as a playful writer who twisted the existing language in magnificent fashion, his contributions to English seem even more phenomenal. Shakespeare is currently the first author for approximately eight thousand different word senses.

This diminished view of the number of words created by Shakespeare should not be taken as an attempt to claim that he didn't have a prodigious vocabulary or that he didn't make enormous contributions to the vocabulary of English. These things are obviously true, but again, they are not quite as true as we suppose.

In addition to captivating innumerable nineteenth-century volunteer readers of the *OED*, Shakespeare managed to attract the attention of another group of antiquarian eccentrics: the language scolds. There was a habit among the grammarians of the eighteenth century to use earlier authors as an example of how even the best writers make mistakes with the language, and Shakespeare provided a gold mine of errors.

Bertil Sundby, in *A Dictionary of English Normative Grammar, 1700–1800*, combed through almost all of the grammar books of the eighteenth century and gave an exhaustive list of writers who were censured by the grammarians. Shakespeare was corrected more than a hundred times by various grammar guides in that century.

In many cases the quibbles about his language use were obviously absurd: Shakespeare was writing at a time before many of the modern rules of language existed, and he would have had no way of knowing that he was going to be violating some rule of the future. Many of these grammarians seemed to view Shakespeare's linguistic fallibility as evidence of universal culpability: If even our greatest writer failed to adhere to the proper rules, then none of us mortals are without sin.

Shakespeare's work abounds with examples of language that, were they used today, would cause any English teacher to tear her hair out. He was quite fond of using not only double negatives* but double comparatives as well.† Again, both of these were not yet condemned in English use, so it's hardly surprising to see them there.

But Shakespeare's "errors," if we can call them that, are not confined simply to violating rules that did not yet exist. He routinely fails to make his verbs and nouns agree, as when Cassius says "Myself have to mine own turn'd enemy" in Act 5 of *Julius Caesar,* or when Ophelia says to Hamlet "And there is pansies, that's for thoughts."

In 1870 the scholar Edwin A. Abbott devoted more than thirty pages of *A Shakespearian Grammar* to what he delicately termed "irregularities."[31] In addition to his doubled comparatives and negatives and his problems with subject–verb agreement, Shake-

----

* "I cannot go no further": *As You Like It* 2.4.

† "More harder than the stones whereof 'tis raised": *King Lear* 3.2.

speare was prone to mashing together Germanic and Latin roots to make Franken-words such as *increaseful*,* doubled up his prepositions (to say nothing of using them to end his sentences),† and routinely used existing words to mean things that they had never meant before.

What would Shakespeare's prose look like if we "corrected" it, at least according to our modern view of what is correct? What if he had had an overzealous copy editor who took out all of his playful use of language, who applied all of the strictures of the most nitpicky grammarians over the past few hundred years? Let's look at the first ten lines of what is perhaps his most famous soliloquy: *Hamlet* Act 3, scene 1. The copy editor's notes and corrections are in parentheses:

> *To be, or not to be: <u>that is the question</u>: (this is a statement, not a question)*
> *Whether 'tis (avoid contractions) nobler in the mind to suffer*
> *The slings and arrows of <u>outrageous</u> (this word is of French origin—can you find one from Anglo-Saxon roots?) <u>fortune</u> (see previous comment, perhaps use Old English* hap *instead of Latinate* fortune?)
> *Or to take arms against <u>a sea of troubles</u>, (avoid metaphors that you are used to seeing in print)*
> *And by opposing end them. To die, to sleep—*
> *No more—and by a sleep to say we end*
> *The heartache, and the thousand natural shocks*

----

* From the Latin *incrēscĕre* and the Old English *full*.

† "In what enormity is Marcius poor in?": *Coriolanus* 2.1.

That flesh is heir <u>to</u>! (do not end sentences with prepositions) 'Tis
(avoid contractions) a <u>consummation</u> (author appears to be
the first one to use this word in this sense—is this a mistake?)
Devoutly to be wished. To die, to sleep—
To sleep—perchance to dream: ay, <u>there's the rub</u> (author is first
to use this expression—what does "there's the rub" mean?)

It is obvious that were we to do this, most of Shakespeare's writing would bear little resemblance to the work that we know and revere today. Although there have been scattered attempts to fix the Bard's language (either as Alexander Pope did, mentioned in Chapter 1, or when Thomas Bowdler published a sanitized version of Shakespeare's works with the naughty parts taken out), for the most part we today accept that the language of our most venerated writer is a bit of a hot mess, and we are just fine with that.

Our relationship with Shakespeare and his language is dichotomous in a way that echoes our relationship with the English language itself. We teach students to never use double negatives or double comparatives, while at the same time we have them study the writing of a man who used both of these freely. Many English teachers refuse to accept semantic drift in words such as *decimate, literally,* and *hopefully,* while instructing their students in the writings of a man for whom *punk* meant "prostitute," and who used the word *learn* to mean "to teach."

An example of how foreign the language of Shakespeare would appear to us today, if we did not know it was Shakespeare's, can be found in George McKnight's 1928 *Modern English in the Making.* McKnight tells a story about a young Syrian man in the early twentieth century who learned to speak English entirely through a study of Shakespeare. Equipped with this fluency, he traveled to London, where he was in short order installed in a mental institution, presumably on the basis of his outlandish speech. McKnight says the story is "supposedly true," but provides no citations or evidence, so it seems just as likely that it is apocryphal.[32] But it is not difficult to imagine that this would be a likely outcome for anyone today who insisted on speaking in Elizabethan English.

In light of Shakespeare's willingness to bend the rules of English, to make a word mean what he wanted it to mean, shouldn't we be willing to accommodate more of this inventive spirit in the language usage of each other? Granted, the people who annoy you with their muddled semantics and misplaced apostrophes are not channeling their inner Bard, and there is no suggestion that unintentional misuse of language should be encouraged. But neither should shaming be used in place of actually explaining the joy and mysteries of how the English language functions.

And so, in honor of the playful nature of so much of Shakespeare's language, I am concluding by offering a quiz. Following are listed ten citations, taken from two disparate worlds: Shakespeare and hip-hop or rap lyrics. The premise is quite simple: read each one and guess whether it comes from the most celebrated author in the history of English or from an almost entirely oral musical form that has received scant recognition from academia or most of the mainstream press. I think the entries provide evidence of the timeless nature of our language, its ability to change and yet remain the same, and that a delight in language need not be hampered by any strict adherence to rules. Read and celebrate (the answers are on page 228).

1. The music, ho!

2. But if you don't, I'll unsheathe my Excalibur, Like a noble knight.

3. Holla, holla!

4. This is the proper way man should use ink.

5. Let's beat him before his whore.

6. Welcome, ass, Now let's have a catch.

7. I live by the sword, I take my boys everywhere I go.

8. Never name her, child, if she be a whore.

9. The money that you owe me for the chain.

10. Pay me back when you shake it again.

11. Holla, ho! Curtis!

12. Sabotaged, Shellshocked, rocked and ruled, Day in the life of a fool.

13. Now the tables turned, but I remember they used to clown me.

14. Every square inch of it, that he chose for himself, is the best part.

seven

221 Words That
Were Once Frowned Upon

Often when I find myself in conversation on the subject of proscriptions about language, a familiar refrain emerges: The person I'm talking with will say, a touch defensively, that while they certainly have no problem with people doing such-and-such, they do draw the line at them doing so-and-so. Unfortunately, no one has ever managed to get the entire population to agree on what exactly is correct and what is incorrect.

So while you may find it perfectly acceptable to use *author* as a verb but find it abhorrent to hear someone say that they *impacted* something, bear in mind that there are others who feel the converse.

What follows is an extremely partial list of words and senses that are now in common (which is not necessarily to say respectable) use and that have been frowned upon at some point in the past few hundred years. Each word has a citation from a usage guide or grammar book, describing what problem the author had with the way the word was used.

Look over the list, and if you find that there are no entries that you would ever deign to use you should perhaps consider relaxing your standards. If, however, you find that you are prone to breaking someone else's rules on correct English usage and some portion of this list overlaps with your own usage, rest assured that this does not mean you have trouble with language. It is merely a testament to your membership in the club of English-speaking people.

Accessorize: "Accessorize is a bastard offshoot of the noun accessory. . . . Avoid accessorize."—William and Mary Morris, *Harper's Dictionary of Contemporary Usage*, 1975

Ad: "This abbreviation for the word advertisement is very justly considered a gross vulgarism. It is doubtful whether it is permissible under any circumstances."—Alfred Ayres, *The Verbalist*, 1894

Administer: "'Carson died from blows *administered* by policeman Johnson.'—*New York Times*. If policeman Johnson was as barbarous as is this use of the verb *to administer*, it is to be hoped that he was hanged. Governments, oaths, medicine, affairs—such as the affairs of the state—are *administered*, but not blows: *they* are *dealt*."—Alfred Ayres, *The Verbalist*, 1894

Ado: "Ado is an Abbreviation of *to do*, and ought never be used by any Man, who has the least Regard for the English Language or his own Credit."—George Harris, *Observations upon the English Language*, 1752

Adore: "Often misused as an emphatic for 'like.' One may *adore* that which one reveres or venerates or has profound regard or affection for, but not that which is pleasant to the palate. A child may *like* cherries and *adore* its mother, but it does not *adore* cherries though it *likes* its mother."—Frank Vizetelly, *Errors in English*, 1906

Affable: "The word 'affable' is used sometimes as though it meant 'polite,' 'courteous,' but such use is incorrect. . . . 'Affable' and 'affability' are used properly only when speaking of the bearing of a superior to one who is socially or otherwise an inferior."—Charles Lurie, *How to Say It: Helpful Hints on English*, 1926

Aggravate: "Aggravate is misused by many persons ignorantly, and in consequence, by many others thoughtlessly, in the sense of provoke, irritate, anger."—Richard Grant White, *Words and Their Uses*, 1882

Ain't: "This contraction is universally condemned."—Robert Palfrey Utter, *Every-Day Words and Their Uses*, 1916

Air: "'Air' in the sense of 'broadcast' is a colloquialism; it is also an unnecessary word."—Theodore Bernstein, *Watch Your Language*, 1958

Alibi: "The easiest and silliest way in which to impoverish the language is to misuse a good existing word that conveys a clear and precise meaning and thereby to destroy that meaning and render the word useless. This is what Americans have done by using 'alibi' when they mean 'excuse.'"—Lord Conesford, "You Americans Are Murdering the Language," *Saturday Evening Post*, 1957

Antagonize: "Strictly, *antagonize* means oppose, and implies nothing as to the effect of the opposition or the opposed: a congressman may *antagonize* a man without *alienating* him . . . note that *antagonism* means *opposition*, not necessarily *animosity*."—H. N. McCracken and Helen Sandison, *Manual of Good English*, 1919

Anticipate: "Lovers of big words have a fondness for making this word do duty for *expect*. . . . It is, therefore, misused in such sentences as . . .

'By this means it is *anticipated* that the time from Europe will be lessened two days.'"—Alfred Ayres, *The Verbalist*, 1894

Anxious: "Anxious for Eager. 'I was anxious to go.' Anxious should not be followed by an infinitive. Anxiety is contemplative; eagerness, alert for action."—Ambrose Bierce, *Write It Right*, 1909

Anyhow: "Any how is an exceedingly vulgar phrase, though used even by so elegant a writer as Blair. . . . The use of this expression, in any manner, by one who professes to write and speak the English tongue with purity, is unpardonable."—William Matthews, *Words, Their Use and Abuse*, 1882

Appreciate: "If any word in the language has cause to complain of ill-treatment, this one has. *Appreciate* means, to estimate *justly*—to set the true value on men or things, their worth, beauty, or advantages of any sort whatsoever . . . hence it follows that such expressions as, 'I appreciate it, or her, or him, *highly*,' can not be correct."—Alfred Ayres, *The Verbalist*, 1894

Aren't I: "Aren't I for am I not is an ungrammatical colloquialism said to be in better standing in England than in the United States."—Robert Palfrey Utter, *Every-Day Words and Their Uses*, 1916

Auto: "An abbreviation not desirable in formal writing."—Garland Greever and Easley Jones, *Century Handbook of Writing*, 1926

Author (v.): "'Authored' is even less acceptable in casual speech than in writing."—George Cornish, in *Harper's Dictionary of Contemporary Usage*, 1975

Authoress: "A needless word—as needless as 'poetess.'"—Ambrose Bierce, *Write It Right*, 1909

Awful: "*Awful* means inspiring with awe. . . . Incorrect uses of this word are found in colloquial speech; as, . . . 'an *awful* dinner.'"—Josephine Turck Baker, *The Correct Word*, 1899

Back talk: "A vulgarism for any impertinent reply; as, 'Don't give me any *back talk*.' Persons of refinement say, 'Don't be impertinent,' or, 'Stop your impertinence.'"—Frank Vizetelly, *Errors in English*, 1906

Bad egg: "An undesirable expression used colloquially to designate a worthless person: not used in polite society."—Frank Vizetelly, *Errors in English*, 1906

Balance: "Balance, in the sense of rest, remainder, residue, remnant, is an abomination."—Richard Grant White, *Words and Their Uses*, 1882

Balding: "There is no such word as 'balding.' Why not 'baldish'?" —Theodore Bernstein, *Watch Your Language*, 1958

Bannister: "There are hundreds of educated persons who speak of the 'banister' of a staircase, when they mean 'balustrade,' or 'baluster'; there is no such word as 'banister.'"—William Matthews, *Words, Their Use and Abuse*, 1882

Beat: "Should not be used for 'defeat.'"—Frank Vizetelly, *Errors in English*, 1906

Blowhard: "A coarse term for 'boaster' synonymous with windbag; not used by persons of refinement."—Frank Vizetelly, *Errors in English*, 1906

Bogus: "A colloquial term incompatible with dignified diction." —Alfred Ayres, *The Verbalist*, 1894

Brainy: "Pure Slang, and singularly disagreeable."—Ambrose Bierce, *Write It Right*, 1909

Brand: "[B]rand is now a commercial term signifying the product of a particular manufacturer, or the kind of quality of a product. It has been extended—at first the extension was semihumorous—to denote a sort or class of anything, as in 'Smith's brand of republicanism.' But there is no need for this kind of extension; many other good words say the same thing."—Theodore Bernstein, *The Careful Writer*, 1965

Broadcasted: "Among other terms, the wireless has introduced 'broadcast' in its newer sense. Many persons, however, are saying and writing 'broadcasted,' which is incorrect. 'Broadcast' is derived from the simpler verb 'cast.' The past form of 'cast' is not 'casted,' but 'cast.' Therefore, the past or participal (*sic*) form of 'broadcast' is not 'broadcasted,' but 'broadcast.'"—Charles Lurie, *How to Say It*, 1926

Bug: "*Bug* for *Beetle*, or for anything. Do not use it."—Ambrose Bierce, *Write It Right*, 1909

Burglarize: "Burglarize is also condemned as a useless invention of newspaper writers. Rob is better."—Robert Palfrey Utter, *Every-Day Words and Their Uses*, 1916

Bureau: "'Bureau' is a misapplied term which curiously crept into our domestic vocabulary, but is being gradually expunged from it. It is not etiquette now to say 'bureau,' except in its proper sense. Applying it to a chest of drawers or a dressing-table is only done in the rural districts now, although it was once a universal habit here."—*Etiquette for Americans (by a Woman of Fashion)*, 1909

Burgle: "'Burgle,' like 'enthuse,' makes every grammarian 'see red' when he hears it used in speech or beholds it on paper. There is no authority for its use, and it should not have a place in the vocabulary of any person who desires to speak and write correctly."—Charles Lurie, *How to Say It*, 1926

Bus: "Bus, as a transitive verb (to bus children), is acceptable in writing to only 48 per cent of the Usage Panel, but in speech to 60 per cent."—*American Heritage Dictionary of the English Language*, 1969

Butt in: "A vulgar although expressive phrase meaning 'to interfere officiously or inquisitively with,' not used by persons accustomed to refined diction."—Frank Vizetelly, *Errors in English*, 1906

Cablegram: "There could not be a finer specimen of an utterly superfluous monster than this English-Greek hybrid *cablegram*."—Richard Grant White, *Words and Their Uses*, 1882

Caliber: "This word is sometimes used very absurdly; as, 'Brown's Essays are of a much higher *caliber* than Smith's.' It is plain that the proper word to use here is *order*."—Alfred Ayres, *The Verbalist*, 1894

Canine: "Should not be used for 'dog.'"—Frank Vizetelly, *Errors in English*, 1906

Caption: "The affectation of fine, big-sounding words which have a flavor of classical learning has had few more laughable or absurd manifestations than the use of *caption* (which means seizure, act of taking), in the sense, and in the rightful place, of *heading*.'"—Richard Grant White, *Words and Their Uses*, 1882

Carnival: "This word literally means 'Farewell to meat,' or, as some etymologists think, 'Flesh, be strong!' . . . In this country it is employed in the sense of fun, frolic, spree, festival; and that so generally as almost to have banished some of these words from the language. . . . As we have plenty of legitimate words to describe these festivities, the use of this outlandish term has not a shadow of justification."—William Matthews, *Words, Their Use and Abuse,* 1882

Casket (meaning "coffin"): "A needless euphemism affected by undertakers."—Ambrose Bierce, *Write It Right,* 1909

Celebrity: "'A number of *celebrities* witnessed the first representation.' This word is frequently used, especially in newspapers, as a concrete term; but it would be better to use it in its abstract sense only, and in sentences like the one above to say *distinguished persons.*"—Alfred Ayres, *The Verbalist,* 1894

Chair (v.): "Chair as a verb meaning serve as chairman is not fully acceptable, in spite of its popularity on the society pages, where some other questionable verbs, such as host, find a haven."—Roy Copperud, *Words on Paper,* 1964

Claim: "A vulgarism that has made its way, probably through the advertising column, into journalism, & is now of daily currency, is the use of *claim* in the sense of *assert, maintain,* or *represent.*"—Henry Fowler, *A Dictionary of Modern English Usage,* 1926

Climax: "The Greek word *climax* means literally a *ladder,* and implies *ascent, upward movement.* The best authors use it only in this sense, and not to denote the highest point."—John Hendricks Bechtel, *Slips of Speech,* 1901

Climb down: "Climb indicates ascension; in consequence, 'climb down' is censured."—Josephine Turck Baker, *The Correct Word,* 1899

Coincidence: "*Coincidence,* implying the co-occurrence of two or more events, cannot refer to one event. Correct: It's a coincidence that they should both come here today. [Not: His arrival here today is a *coincidence.*]"—H. N. McCracken and Helen Sandison, *Manual of Good English*, 1919

Collide: "For a collision, from Latin *col* + *laedere*, to strike together, at least two objects must be in motion. Thus, a moving vehicle doesn't collide with a parked vehicle or some other stationary object."—John Bremner, *Words on Words*, 1980

Commence: "Begin. A good plain Saxon word, understood and felt by learned and unlearned alike, almost always to be preferred to the French *commense.*"—Funk and Wagnalls, *Faulty Diction*, 1917

Con man: "A vulgar term for a swindler's decoy or 'bunco-steerer'; a *confidence man*: not used in polite society."—Frank Vizetelly, *Errors in English*, 1906

Consequential: "Consequential does not mean of consequence; a consequential person may or may not be important; all we know is that he is self-important."—Henry Fowler and Ernest Gowers, *A Dictionary of Modern English Usage*, 1965

Consider: "*Consider* is perverted from its true meaning by most of those who use it. Men will say that they do not consider a certain course of conduct right or politic . . . and even that they do not consider gooseberry tart equal to strawberry short-cake. Now, *considere* (the infinitive of *consido*) on which consider is formed, means to sit down deliberately, to dwell upon, to hold a sitting, to sit in judgement; and hence *consider*, by natural process came to mean, to ponder, to contemplate. . . . All this fine and useful sense of the word is lost by making it a mere synonyme of think, suppose, or regard."—Richard Grant White, *Words and Their Uses*, 1882

Counterproductive: "Counterproductive says nothing that self-defeating doesn't say quite as well."—William and Mary Morris, *Harper's Dictionary of Contemporary Usage*, 1975

Couple: "Although the misuse of this word is very common, and of long standing, the perversion of meaning in the misuse is so great that it cannot be justified, even by time and custom. It is used to mean simply two; as, for instance, 'A couple of ladies fell upon the ice yesterday afternoon.' . . . It is as incorrect and as absurd to speak of a couple of ladies, or a couple of prizes, as of a couple of earthquakes or a couple of comets."—Richard Grant White, *Words and Their Uses*, 1882

Craft: "I don't admire the use of 'craft' as a verb in any context." —Dwight Macdonald, in *Harper's Dictionary of Contemporary Usage*, 1975

Critique: "Critique is in less common use than it was, &, with *review, criticism,* & *notice,* ready at need, there is some hope of its dying out."—Henry Fowler, *A Dictionary of Modern English Usage*, 1926

Date: "*Date* is incorrectly used in the sense of an *engagement*; as, 'I have a *date* this evening,' instead of 'I have an *engagement* this evening.'" —Josephine Turck Baker, *The Correct Word*, 1899

Deal: "*Deal*, in the sense of *transaction, agreement,* or *arrangement,* is incorrect."—Josephine Turck Baker, *The Correct Word*, 1899

Debut: "A good noun, a lousy verb, whether transitive . . . or intransitive."—John Bremner, *Words on Words*, 1980

Decimate: "But to use decimation as a general phrase for great slaughter is simply ridiculous."—Richard Grant White, *Words and Their Uses*, 1882

Demean: "Means *to conduct oneself,* not *to lower* or *to degrade.*"—Garland Greever and Easley Jones, *Century Handbook of Writing*, 1926

Despicable: "Cannot be excused in my opinion for smellynge to much of the Latine"*—Richard Willes, *The History of Trauayle*, 1577

Dilapidated (meaning "run-down"): "[T]he word is from the Latin *lapis*, a stone, and cannot properly be used of any but a stone building." —Ambrose Bierce, *Write It Right*, 1909

Directly: "As a quasi-conjunction in the sense of *as soon as*; . . . a common but objectionable British colloquialism, introduced to some extent into the United States."—Funk and Wagnalls, *Faulty Diction*, 1917

Dirt (meaning "soil or earth"): "A most disagreeable Americanism . . . dirt means filth."—Ambrose Bierce, *Write It Right*, 1909

Discomfit: "There is a tendency to sue this is too weak or indefinite a sense. . . . It is perhaps mistaken sometimes for the verb belonging to the noun *discomfort*. It has nothing to do with that, & means overwhelm or utterly defeat."—Henry Fowler, *A Dictionary of Modern English Usage*, 1926

Dock: "Dock is by many persons used to mean a wharf or pier; thus: He fell off the dock, and was drowned. A dock is an open place without a roof, into which anything is received, and where it is enclosed for safety. . . . A man might fall into a dock; but to say that he fell off a dock is no better than to say that he fell off a hole."—Richard Grant White, *Words and Their Uses*, 1882

Donate: "Don't say *donate* when you mean *give*. The use of this pretentious word for every instance of giving has become so common as to

---

* *Smellyng to much of the Latine* was the turn of phrase Willes used to describe words he thought were preposterous Latinisms.

be fairly nauseating. . . . If one can not give his church or town library a little money without calling it *donating,* let him, in the name of good English, keep his gift until he has learned better."—Oliver Bell Bunce, *Don't,* 1884

Done: "The word should not be used in good writing to mean finished or completed."—Theodore Bernstein, *The Careful Writer,* 1965

Drapes: "Never say drapes. . . . Say instead curtains, or, if necessary, draperies. ('Drapes' is seen in the advertising pages every day, but it is still a flagrant example of bad taste.)"—Emily Post, *Etiquette: The Blue Book of Social Usage,* 1945

Dress: "Within the memory of many persons the outer garment worn by women was properly called a *gown* by everybody, instead of being improperly called a *dress,* as it now is by nearly everybody."—Alfred Ayres, *The Verbalist,* 1894

Dumb: "*Dumb* means primarily *unable to speak*; secondarily, *reticent.* Since a person 'who hasn't a word to say for himself' easily gets the reputation of being stupid, and since the German word *dumm* does mean stupid, *dumb* has come into local and vulgar use in the United States to mean *stupid.* All Authorities condemn its use in this sense." —Robert Palfrey Utter, *Every-Day Words and Their Uses,* 1916

Editorial: "An unpleasant Americanism."—Richard Grant White, *Words and Their Uses,* 1882

Educational: "Hideous adjective."—James Fitzjames Stephen, *Essays by a Barrister,* 1862

Electrocution: "[T]o one having even an elementary knowledge of Latin grammar this word is no less than disgusting, and the thing meant by it is felt to be altogether too good for the word's inventor."—Ambrose Bierce, *Write It Right*, 1909

Encounter: "No matter what I had innocently believed all my life, the verb *to encounter* does not mean simply 'to run across.' It means to meet as an adversary or enemy; to engage in conflict with; to run into a complication."—James Kilpatrick, *The Writer's Art*, 1984

Endorse: "[Y]ou may endorse a check, but you approve a policy, or statement."—Ambrose Bierce, *Write It Right*, 1909

End up: "Unacceptable colloquialism for *end* or *conclude*."—*The Macmillan Handbook of English*, 1965

Enormity: "Authorities on usage are virtually unanimous in reserving 'enormity' for the idea of wickedness."—Theodore Bernstein, *Watch Your Language*, 1958

Enthuse: "This ridiculous word is an Americanism in vogue in the southern part of the United States."—Richard Grant White, *Words and Their Uses*, 1882

Escalate: "*Escalate*, a recent BACK-FORMATION from *escalator* (both originally U.S.) was not needed; *escalade* (n. and vb.) has long been in similar metaphorical use. But *-ate* is likely to drive *-ade* out; it has the advantage of novelty and a more native look."—Henry Fowler and Ernest Gowers, *A Dictionary of Modern English Usage*, 1965

Estimation: "The use of *in my* &c. *estimation* as a mere substitution for *in my* &c. *opinion* where there is no question of calculating amounts or degrees . . . is illiterate."—Henry Fowler, *A Dictionary of Modern English Usage*, 1926

Evince: "This 'evince,' by the way, is one of the most odious words in all the catalogue of vulgarities."—Henry Alford, *A Plea for the Queen's English*, 1864

Executed: "A vicious use of this word have prevailed so long, become so common, that, although it produces sheer nonsense, there is little hope of its reformation, except in case of that rare occurrence in the history of language, a vigorous and persistent effort on the part of the best speakers and writers and professional teachers toward the accomplishment of a special purpose. The perversion referred to is the use of *executed* to mean hanged, beheaded, put to death."—Richard Grant White, *Words and Their Uses*, 1882

Expect: "The misuse of the word as a synonym of *suppose*, without any notion of 'anticipating' or 'looking for,' is often cited as an Americanism, but is very common in dialectal, vulgar or carelessly colloquial speech in England."—*Oxford English Dictionary*, 1933

Experience: "Now, in the best English, *experience* is a substantive, *not a verb at all.*"—Henry Alford, *A Plea for the Queen's English*, 1864

Fabulous: "One may properly speak of the fabulous wealth of an impostor, meaning the property that he falsely pretends to have. But what nonsense it is, when one thinks of it, to say that a lady's jewels are of 'fabulous value,' meaning that they cost a great deal of money!"—Gilbert Tucker, *Our Common Speech*, 1895

Fail: "Used carelessly on the college campus in 'I *failed* the course,' and quite improperly in 'He *failed* me in English,' The *student* does the failing, and fails *in* his work."—H. N. McCracken and Helen Sandison, *Manual of Good English*, 1919

Fault: "When used as a transitive verb, *fault* has become a vogue word and as such is greatly overused as a substitute for 'blame' or 'criticize,' either of which is preferable."—William and Mary Morris, *Harper's Dictionary of Contemporary Usage*, 1975

Feature (v.): "The use of this in cinema announcements instead of *represent* or *exhibit* is perhaps from America. . . . Wherever it comes from, it is to be feared that from the cinema bills it will make its way into popular use, which would be a pity."—Henry Fowler, *A Dictionary of Modern English Usage*, 1926

Figurehead: "Often misapplied to people . . . unintentionally demeaning."—Roy Copperud, *American Usage and Style*, 1980

Finalize: "I have noticed that the kind of people who use this atrocious word are often the same people who refer to your letter of, say, the 12th '*ult.*' or '*inst.*' or make an appointment for the 14th '*prox.*,' although the odds are that they haven't the faintest idea what the Latin words *ultimo, instantem,* and *proximo* mean."—John Moore, *You English Words*, 1961

Fine: "Fine better not be used as an adverb. Not 'I like it *fine.*' And do not answer 'How are you?' with 'I am *fine.*'"—Gertrude Payne, *Everyday Errors*, 1911

Finesse: "[A]n unnecessary word which is creeping into the language."—Samuel Johnson, *A Dictionary of the English Language*, 1755

Fix: "Don't use *fix* in the sense of putting in order, setting to rights, etc."—Oliver Bell Bunce, *Don't*, 1884

Flummox: "A vulgarism sometimes used for 'perplex' or 'disconcert.'"—Frank Vizetelly, *Errors in English*, 1906

Forecasted: "For this abominable word we are indebted to the weather bureau. . . . Let us hope that it may some day be losted from the language."—Ambrose Bierce, *Write It Right*, 1909

For free: "The phrases *for free* and *for real* are slang and are used only facetiously by careful writers."—William and Mary Morris, *Harper's Dictionary of Contemporary Usage*, 1975

Forget it: "When used as the equivalent of 'don't talk about it,' it is a vulgarism that can not be too severely condemned."—Frank Vizetelly, *Errors in English*, 1906

Fortuitous: "'Fortuitous' means 'happening by chance'; it does not mean fortunate."—Theodore Herbert, *Watch Your Language*, 1958

Fruition: "Fruition, often wrongly supposed to be associated with the English word fruit, is the enjoyment that comes from the fructification of hope, especially from possession."—Henry Fowler and Ernest Gowers, *A Dictionary of Modern English Usage*, 1965

Fun: "A respectable noun, a slovenly adjective."—John Bremner, *Words on Words*, 1980

Funny: "Don't adopt the common habit of calling everything *funny* that chances to be a little odd or strange."—Oliver Bell Bunce, *Don't*, 1884

Gall: "Correctly used is 'an intensely bitter feeling.' When used as a synonym for 'cool assurance' or 'impudence' it is slang and should be avoided."—Frank Vizetelly, *Errors in English*, 1906

Gender: "[A] grammatical term only. To talk of *persons* or *creatures of the masculine* or *feminine gender*, meaning *of the masculine* or *feminine sex* is either a jocularity (permissible or not according to context) or a blunder."—Henry Fowler, *A Dictionary of Modern English Usage*, 1926

Gent: "Don't say *gents* for *gentlemen*, nor *pants* for *pantaloons*. These are inexcusable vulgarisms."—Oliver Bell Bunce, *Don't*, 1884

Graduate: "Students do not graduate; they are graduated."—Alfred Ayres, *The Verbalist*, 1894

Groom: "Groom should not be used for bridegroom."—Frank Vizetelly, *Errors in English*, 1906

Gubernatorial: "This clumsy piece of verbal pomposity should be thrust out of use, and that speedily."—Richard Grant White, *Words and Their Uses*, 1882

Happening (n.): "It is a Vogue-Word, which has had a startlingly rapid success, & which many of us hope to see wither away as quickly as it has grown."—Henry Fowler, *A Dictionary of Modern English Usage*, 1926

Headquarter: "The use of *headquarter* as a verb, though accepted by some dictionaries as standard and labeled informal by others, can still cause careful users of the language to shudder."—William and Mary Morris, *Harper's Dictionary of Contemporary Usage*, 1975

Healthy: "Don't speak of this or that kind of food being *healthy* or *unhealthy*; say always *wholesome* or *unwholesome*."—Oliver Bell Bunce, *Don't*, 1884

Hectic: "This word, 'hectic,' seems to have become, in recent years, a favorite with writers of many sorts, especially those who treat of baseball, football and other sports. But almost all of them, if not all, use it incorrectly. They believe it to mean 'feverish,' but they are wrong. . . . 'Hectic' means 'habitual or constitutional; denoting a wasting habit or condition of the body; as, a hectic fever, one that consumes the body.' The incorrect use of 'hectic,' noted above as meaning 'feverish,' arose from the medical expression, 'hectic fever.'"—Charles Lurie, *How to Say It*, 1926

Homicide: "[C]annot be excused in my opinion for smellynge to much of the Latine"—Richarde Willes, *The History of Trauayle*, 1577

Honeymoon: "Moon here means month, so it is incorrect to say, 'a week's honeymoon.'"—Ambrose Bierce, *Write It Right*, 1909

Hopefully: "*Hopefully*, as used to mean it is to be hoped or let us hope, is still not accepted by a substantial number of authorities on grammar and usage."—*American Heritage Dictionary of the English Language*, 1969

Hospitalize: "'Hopsitalise,' as the literate know, is no more capable of meaning 'send to a hospital' than 'canalise' is of meaning 'throw into a canal.'"—Lord Conesford, "You Americans Are Murdering the Language," *Saturday Evening Post*, 1957

Host: "As a verb, host is not acceptable ('The East Side Club hosted the convention') although society writers love it. Host may well be left to them, together with chair as a verb."—Roy Copperud, *Words on Paper*, 1960

Human: "Not in good use as a noun. Say *human being*."—Garland Greever and Easley Jones, *Century Handbook of Writing*, 1926

Humanitarian: "Humanitarian is very strangely perverted by a certain class of speakers and writers. It is a theological word; and its original meaning is, One who denies the godhead of Jesus Christ, and insists upon his human nature."—Richard Grant White, *Words and Their Uses*, 1882

Hurry: "Though widely different in meaning, both the verb and the noun *hurry* are continually used for *haste* and *hasten*. *Hurry* implies not only *haste*, but haste with confusion, flurry . . . sensible people, then, may be often in *haste*, but are never in a *hurry*; and we tell others to *make haste,* and not to *hurry up.*"—Alfred Ayres, *The Verbalist,* 1894

Ice cream: "By mere carelessness in enunciation these compound words have come to be used for *iced-water* and *iced-cream*—most incorrectly and with a real confusion of language, if not of thought." —Richard Grant White, *Words and Their Uses,* 1882

Impact: "Impact is not a verb."—Brian Ross-Larson, *Edit Yourself,* 1996

Inaugurate: "Inaugurate is a word which might better be eschewed by all those who do not wish to talk high-flying nonsense, else they will find themselves led by bad example into using it in the sense of begin, open, set up, establish. . . . To inaugurate is to receive or induct into office with solemn ceremonies."—Richard Grant White, *Words and Their Uses,* 1882

Individual: "*Individual* properly means, as most commonly used, a single human being *as opposed to Society, or to some group, as family or church.* As meaning simply a *person* it is colloquial, vulgar, or humorous."—Robert Palfrey Utter, *Every-Day Words and Their Uses,* 1916

Initiate: "This is a pretentious word, which, with its derivatives, many persons—especially those who like to be grandiloquent—use, when homely English would serve their turn much better."—Alfred Ayres, *The Verbalist,* 1894

Interface: "What's wrong with 'interact'? When I interface with a girl, I'm *kissing* her, by God."—Isaac Asimov, in *Harper's Dictionary of Contemporary Usage,* 1985

Invite: "A needless barbarism, since we have the correct and established term *invitation.*"—Funk and Wagnalls, *Faulty Diction,* 1917

It's: "It's for it is is vulgar; 'tis is used."—James Buchanan, *A Regular English Syntax*, 1767

Jar: "Used in the phrase 'Doesn't (or wouldn't) it jar you' is an erroneous use of the word *jar* in vogue among people addicted to using the vulgarisms of the street. To jar is 'to cause to shake as by a shock or blow; to jolt'; *not*, to disconcert or discompose."—Frank Vizetelly, *Errors in English*, 1906

Jeopardize: "Among the monsters in this form none is more frequently met with than *jeopardize*—a foolish and intolerable word, which has no rightful place in the language."—Richard Grant White, *Words and Their Uses*, 1882

Kid: "A common vulgarism for 'child' and as such one the use of which can not be too severely condemned."—Frank Vizetelly, *Errors in English*, 1906

Kind: "Kind of is an American provincialism for *somewhat* and has no literary authorization."—Frank Vizetelly, *Errors in English*, 1906

Lady-friend: "The expressions, 'my gentleman-friend'—'my lady-friend,' are vulgarisms."—Richard Meade Bache, *Vulgarisms and Other Errors of Speech*, 1868

Lawmen: "What on earth are 'lawmen' and what is the need for such a coinage?"—Theodore Bernstein, *Watch Your Language*, 1958

Leave: "This verb is very commonly ill used by being left without an object. Thus: Jones left this morning; I shall leave this evening. Left what? shall leave what? Not the morning or the evening, but home, town, or country. When this verb is used, the mention of the place referred to is absolutely necessary."—Richard Grant White, *Words and Their Uses*, 1882

Lengthy: "It is no better than breadthy, or thicknessy."—Ambrose Bierce, *Write It Right*, 1909

Leniency: "This is a word—if, as previously suggested, it deserves to be called a 'word'—which is not needed in our language;—which is not justified by the precedents of our language;—which did not originate with educated men;—and which should not receive the sanction of educated men."—Edward S. Gould, *Good English*, 1880

Lesser: "A barbarous corruption of less, formed by the vulgar from the habit of terminating comparatives in er; afterwards adopted by poets, and then by writers of prose."—Samuel Johnson, *A Dictionary of the English Language*, 1755

Like: "Like is never a conjunction."—H. N. McCracken and Helen Sandison, *Manual of Good English*, 1919

Literally: "Do not use it when you plainly do not mean it, as in the sentence, 'I was literally tickled to death.'"—Garland Greever and Easley Jones, *Century Handbook of Writing*, 1926

Loan: "Loan is not a verb, but a noun."—Richard Grant White, *Words and Their Uses*, 1882

Lots: "Don't say 'lots of things,' meaning 'an abundance of things.' A *lot* of anything means a separate portion, a part allotted."—Oliver Bell Bunce, *Don't*, 1884

Lovely: "*Lovely* is properly used only of that which is worthy of love; in consequence, it should not be used in such expression as, 'The dinner was *lovely*.'"—Josephine Turck Baker, *The Correct Word*, 1899

Lunch: "Luncheon is the preferred form of the noun, *lunch* being properly restricted to express action."—Josephine Turck Baker, *The Correct Word*, 1899

Mad: "Don't use *mad* for *angry*."—Oliver Bell Bunce, *Don't*, 1884

Make: "Used with excessive frequency for *earn*, *gain*, etc.; as, 'How much did he *make*?' . . . Such colloquialisms should not be allowed to crowd out more exact and unobjectionable phrases."—Funk and Wagnalls, *Faulty Diction*, 1917

Mansion: "Never say mansion. . . . Say instead big house."—Emily Post, *Etiquette*, 1945

Marry: "'She married a man named Brown,' is incorrect. . . . A woman, when she weds, is married to a man, but the clergyman or magistrate marries her."—Josephine Turck Baker, *The Correct Word*, 1899

Materialize: "To materialize, to burglarize, to enthuse, to suicide, to wire, to jump upon, to sit upon, to take in, are a few of the many examples of slang that should be avoided."—John Hendricks Bechtel, *Slips of Speech*, 1901

Mean: "A word often erroneously used. . . . In the United States it is commonly misused as a substitute for 'ill-tempered; disagreeable.'"—Frank Vizetelly, *Errors in English*, 1906

Meat: "At table, we ask for and offer beef, mutton, veal, steak, turkey, duck, etc., and do not ask for nor offer *meat*, which, to say the least, is inelegant."—Alfred Ayres, *The Verbalist*, 1894

Mistaken: "'You are mistaken.' For whom? Say, You mistake."—Ambrose Bierce, *Write It Right*, 1909

Momentarily: "Momentarily, momently. . . . The differentiation is well worth more faithful observance than it gets, & the substitution of either, which sometimes occurs, for *instantly* or *immediately* or *at once* is foolish NOVELTY-HUNTING."—Henry Fowler, *A Dictionary of Modern English Usage*, 1926

Mortician: "Never say mortician. . . . Say instead funeral director."
—Emily Post, *Etiquette*, 1945

Nasty: "This word should not be applied to that which is merely 'disagreeable,' as nasty weather, for strong terms should not be robbed of their significance by being applied to conditions which could only be referred to in such terms by exaggeration."—Frank Vizetelly, *Errors in English*, 1906

Nerve: "A slang term sometimes used as a substitute for 'impudence,' 'over-assurance' or 'independence,' any one of which is preferable."
—Frank Vizetelly, *Errors in English*, 1906

Nice: "Improperly used to express every kind and degree of admired or appreciated quality; as, 'a *nice* time,' 'a *nice* horse,' 'a *nice* rain,' 'a *nice* man,' 'a *nice* sermon,' 'a *nice* funeral.'"—Funk and Wagnalls, *Faulty Diction*, 1917

Nicely: "The very quintessence of popinjay vulgarity is reached when *nicely* is made to do service for *well*."—Alfred Ayres, *The Verbalist*, 1894

None: "None is a contraction of no one, and therefore to say 'none are,' or 'none were,' is just as improper as to say 'no one are,' or 'no one were.'"—William Matthews, *Words, Their Use and Abuse*, 1882

Normalcy: "Normalcy (= *normality*) is a Hybrid Derivative of the 'spurious hybrid' class, & seems to have nothing to recommend it."
—Henry Fowler, *A Dictionary of Modern English Usage*, 1926

Notice: "Notice should not be used as a verb. The proper phrase is take notice."—J. Johnson, *The New Royal and Universal English Dictionary*, 1762

Obnoxious: "Obnoxious means exposed to evil. A soldier in battle is obnoxious to danger."—Ambrose Bierce, *Write It Right*, 1909

Oh my: "Don't use meaningless exclamations, such as 'Oh, my!' 'Oh, Crackey!' etc."—Oliver Bell Bunce, *Don't*, 1884

Older: "*Older* is properly applied to objects, animate and inanimate; *elder*, to rational beings."—William Matthews, *Words, Their Use and Abuse*, 1882

Ovation: "In ancient Rome an ovation was an inferior triumph accorded to victors in minor wars or unimportant battle. Its character and limitations, like those of the triumph, were strictly defined by law and custom. An enthusiastic demonstration in honor of an American civilian is nothing like that, and should not be called by its name."—Ambrose Bierce, *Write It Right*, 1909

Overall: "In about nine cases out of ten, the word now bears no meaning whatever and can be omitted without affecting the sense in any way. In the tenth case, the meaning may be 'total,' 'average,' 'overriding,' 'complete' or any one of several other things."—Lord Conesford, "You Americans Are Murdering the Language," *Saturday Evening Post*, 1957

Overly: "This word is now used only by the unschooled."—Alfred Ayres, *The Verbalist*, 1894

Pants: "Abbreviated from pantaloons, which are no longer worn. Vulgar exceedingly."—Ambrose Bierce, *Write It Right*, 1909

Paraphernalia: "The constant misuse of this word has caused it almost entirely to lose its original signification. It is a law-term and only a law-term, originally; and it so continues."—Edward S. Gould, *Good English*, 1880

Parent: "I suspect 'to parent' is yet another manifestation of the Women's Lib assault on the language."—Alex Faulkner, in *Harper's Dictionary of Contemporary Usage*, 1985

Per day: "If you must use the Latin preposition use the Latin noun too: *per diem*."—Ambrose Bierce, *Write It Right*, 1909

Phone: "A contraction not employed in formal writing. Say *telephone*."—Garland Greever and Easley Jones, *Century Handbook of Writing*, 1926

Photo: "Never say photo, auto, mints (All abbreviated words should be avoided, but business has gradually lessened the tabu against phone—except for those who have no 'business custom' excuse.). . . . Say instead telephone, photograph, automobile (or motor), peppermints."—Emily Post, *Etiquette*, 1945

Photographer: "*Er*, the Anglo-Saxon sign of the doer of a thing, is incorrectly affixed to such words as *photograph* and *telegraph*, which should give us *photographist* and *telegraphist*."—Richard Grant White, *Words and Their Uses*, 1882

Polite: "This word is much used by persons of doubtful culture, where those of the better sort use the word *kind*. We accept *kind*, not *polite* invitations."—Alfred Ayres, *The Verbalist*, 1894

Ponderous: "[C]annot be excused in my opinion for smellynge to much of the Latine"—Richarde Willes, *The History of Trauayle*, 1577

Portion: "*Portion* is commonly misused in the sense of *part*. . . . A portion is a part set aside for a special purpose, or to be considered by itself."—Richard Grant White, *Words and Their Uses*, 1882

Practically: "Avoid the word when it synonymizes *almost* or *virtually*—*as good as*—*to all intents*—*in effect*—*though not formally* (or *explicitly*), and select whichever of those seven synonyms is the most suitable to the context."—Eric Partridge, *Usage and Abusage*, 1969

Practitioner: "Practitioner is an unlovely intruder, which has slipped into the English language through the physician's gate."—Richard Grant White, *Words and Their Uses*, 1882

Premiere: "I think 'premiere' as a verb is barbarous, transitive or intransitive. The same is true of 'debut.' These are verbs wrenched from their respectable origins as nouns."—Stewart Beach, in *Harper's Dictionary of Contemporary Usage*, 1985

Present: "The use of this word for *introduce* is an affectation."—Richard Grant White, *Words and Their Uses*, 1882

Presidential: "This adjective, which is used among us now more frequently than any other not vituperative, laudatory, or boastful, is not a legitimate word."—Richard Grant White, *Words and Their Uses*, 1882

Preventative: "No such word as preventative."—Ambrose Bierce, *Write It Right*, 1909

Progress: "Much ink has been wasted to prove that progress, as a verb, is both an Americanism and a modern vulgarism."—Edward S. Gould, *Good English*, 1880

Proposition: "There's no such verb."—Theodore Bernstein, *Watch Your Language*, 1958

Proven: "Proven, which is frequently used now by lawyers and journalists, should, perhaps, be ranked among words that are not words. . . . *Proved* is the past participle of the verb *to prove*, and should be used by all who wish to speak English."—Richard Grant White, *Words and Their Uses*, 1882

Protagonist: "The Greek *protagonistes* means the actor who takes the chief part in a play—a sense readily admitting of figurative applica-

tion to the most conspicuous personage in any affair. The deuter-
agonist & tritagonist take parts of second and third importance, &
to talk of several protagonists, or of a chief protagonist or the like,
is an absurdity as great, to anyone who knows Greek, as to call a man
the protagonist of a cause or of a person, instead of the protagonist
of a drama or of an affair."—Henry Fowler, *A Dictionary of Modern
English Usage*, 1926

Purchase: "This word is much preferred to its synonym *buy*, by that
class of people who prefer the word *reside* to *live*, *procure* to *get*, *inaugurate* to *begin*, and so on. They are generally of those who are great
in pretense."—Alfred Ayres, *The Verbalist*, 1894

Real estate: "Real estate is a compound that has no proper place in
the language of every-day life, where it is merely a pretentious intruder from the technical province of law."—Richard Grant White,
Words and Their Uses, 1882

Realtor: "Never say realtor. . . . Say instead real-estate agent."—Emily
Post, *Etiquette*, 1945

Recollect: "Recollect is used by many persons wrongly for *remember*."
—Richard Grant White, *Words and Their Uses*, 1882

Reliable: "*Reliable* is hardly legitimate. . . . '*Trustworthy*' conveys all the
meaning required."—Henry Alford, *A Plea for the Queen's English*, 1864

Revolt: "The use of this word as a transitive verb, although supported
by high authority, is not favored. 'This *revolts* me' is far better expressed by 'This is *revolting* to me.'"—Frank Vizetelly, *Errors in English*,
1906

Rotten: "Everyone knows the proper meaning and use of the word,
and it is not necessary to go into it in detail here. The word should
be restricted to such meaning and use, and should not be employed

in the sense of 'bad,' or 'very bad,' 'poor' or 'very poor.'"—Charles Lurie, *How to Say It*, 1926

Sappy: "An undesirable colloquialism for 'weakly sentimental; silly.'"—Frank Vizetelly, *Errors in English*, 1906

Shamefaced: "Shamefaced, as every reader of Archbishop Trench's books on English knows, is a mere corruption of *shamefast*, a word of the *steadfast* sort."—Richard Grant White, *Words and Their Uses*, 1882

Sick: "Don't say *sick* except when nausea is meant. Say *ill, unwell, indisposed*."—Oliver Bell Bunce, *Don't*, 1884

Slob: "A vulgar equivalent for 'a careless, negligent and incompetent person,' and as such one to be avoided."—Frank Vizetelly, *Errors in English*, 1906

So: "*So* should not be used for *very*; thus, instead of 'I am *so* tired,' one properly says, 'I am *very* tired.'" Josephine Turck Baker, *The Correct Word*, 1899

Splendid: *Splendid* is properly applied to a great career . . . such expressions as 'a *splendid* gown,' 'a *splendid* dinner,' are objectionable." —Josephine Turck Baker, *The Correct Word*, 1899

Standpoint: "But of all the instances in which solemn philological blundering has recently developed itself, *stand-point* stands forth as the bright particular star."—Edward S. Gould, *Good English*, 1880

Store: "The word 'store' for 'shop' is grossly incorrect; and so is 'depot' for 'station.'"—*Etiquette for Americans (by a Woman of Fashion)*, 1909

Supplement: "Supplement, used as a verb. There is considerable authority for this use of the word; but it is a case where usage is clearly opposed to the very principles of the language."—William Matthews, *Words, Their Use and Abuse*, 1882

Talented: "I regret to see that vile and barbarous vocable *talented*, stealing out of the newspapers into the leading reviews and most respectable publications of the day. Why not shillinged, farthinged, tenpenced, &c.?"—Samuel Taylor Coleridge, *Specimens of the Table Talk*, 1835

Tasty: "Although the words tasty and tastily have been used by some good writers, they have at present a decidedly vulgar twang."—Richard Meade Bache, *Vulgarisms and Other Errors of Speech*, 1868

Telegram: "This word, which is claimed as an 'American' production, has taken root quickly, and is probably well fixed in the language. It is both superfluous and incorrectly formed."—Richard Grant White, *Words and Their Uses*, 1882

Thanks: "There are many persons who think it in questionable taste to use *thanks* for *thank you*."—Alfred Ayres, *The Verbalist*, 1894

Through: "The use of the word 'through' in the sense of 'finished' or 'completed' is condemned by virtually all authorities on English, as a vulgarism."—Charles Lurie, *How to Say It*, 1926

Transpire: "Don't say *transpire* when you mean *occur*."—Oliver Bell Bunce, *Don't*, 1884

Unbeknownst: "Provincial error for *without (my) knowledge*."—H. N. McCracken and Helen Sandison, *Manual of Good English*, 1919

Underhanded: "This corruption has not yet made its appearance in newspapers and dictionaries, but it is very common in the conversation of a certain class of people."—Edward S. Gould, *Good English*, 1880

Underprivileged: "Let me pass from American murder to American pretentious illiteracy; from the destruction of an old word to the invention of a new word which clearly cannot bear the meaning assigned to it. 'Underprivileged' is the leading example."—Lord Conesford, "You Americans Are Murdering the Language," *Saturday Evening Post*, 1957

Upcoming: "*Upcoming* has substantially less standing than its synonyms *coming*, *forthcoming* and *approaching*, especially on a formal level." —*American Heritage Dictionary of the English Language*, 1969

Utilize: "Utilize, utilization are, 99 times out of 100, much inferior to *use*, v. and n.; the one other time it is merely inferior."—Eric Partridge, *Usage and Abusage*, 1969

Vest: "Don't say *vest* for *waistcoat*."—Oliver Bell Bunce, *Don't*, 1884

Witness: "[D]ebased to + 'to *see*.' To *witness* is not merely to *see*, but to *testify*, or by being a spectator to be in a position to testify."—Eric Partridge, *Usage and Abusage*, 1969

Wouldn't: "*Wouldn't want* is always incorrect in the first person, 'I *shouldn't* want' being the correct form."—Josephine Turck Baker, *The Correct Word*, 1899

Zoom: "'Zoom,' an aviation term, concerns only upward mobility." —Theodore Bernstein, *Watch Your Language*, 1958

acknowledgments

Thanks are due, as always, to Marian Lizzi, who is everything in an editor that an author could hope for, and to Lauren Becker, who also provided invaluable assistance. Thanks as well to Jim Rutman, who was considerably more involved in the creation of this book than any agent has a need to be, and who improved it through this involvement.

And thanks, and more, are due to my wife, Alexandra Horowitz, who suffered through many months of grammatical questions and observations from me, offered sage advice, and made writing this book (and all else) feel more worth the while.

further reading

There is a large volume of material available to the person who seeks to learn more about how the English language functions. For those who are interested in questions of usage there is no greater resource than *Merriam-Webster's Dictionary of English Usage*. This is a tremendously scholarly work, yet is written in a manner that is easy to understand, no mean feat.

For those who eschew paper and prefer to go to the Internet for guidance, the site Language Log (languagelog.ldc.upenn.edu/nll) provides in-depth analysis of all matters linguistic. Most of the posts are written by linguists, so there is a certain amount of technical jargon, but it is nonetheless well worth visiting. The *Oxford English Dictionary* stands alone as a historical record of our language. The online format (oed.com) also has a search function that is far superior to that of any other dictionary, allowing users to comb through the entire dictionary in search of specific words, authors, and phrases. Online access to this dictionary is available through most libraries.

On the prescriptive side of the aisle, I have found Bryan Garner's *Modern American Usage* to be the most informative and engaging book to consult. It is well written, abounds with illustrative citations, and covers a wide territory. While I reject his premise (prescribing how people should and should not use their language), I must admit that he presents it uncommonly well.

ANSWERS TO SHAKESPEARE QUIZ

1. The music, ho! (Shakespeare, *Antony and Cleopatra*)

2. But if you don't, I'll unsheathe my Excalibur, Like a noble knight. (Gangstarr, "Step in the Arena")

3. Holla, holla! (Shakespeare, *King Lear*)

4. This is the proper way man should use ink. (Big Daddy Kane, "Taste of Chocolate")

5. Let's beat him before his whore. (Shakespeare, *Henry IV, Part 2*)

6. Welcome, ass, Now let's have a catch. (Shakespeare, *Twelfth Night*)

7. I live by the sword, I take my boys everywhere I go. (Geto Boys, "Mind Playing Tricks on Me")

8. Never name her, child, if she be a whore. (Shakespeare, *Merry Wives of Windsor*)

9. The money that you owe me for the chain. (Shakespeare, *Comedy of Errors*)

10. Pay me back when you shake it again. (Nas, "You Owe Me")

11. Holla, ho! Curtis! (Shakespeare, *Taming of the Shrew*)

12. Sabotaged, Shellshocked, rocked and ruled, Day in the life of a fool. (Public Enemy, "Brothers Gonna Work It Out")

13. Now the tables turned, but I remember they used to clown me. (Mack 10 and Gerald Levert, "Money's Just a Touch Away")

14. Every square inch of it, that he chose for himself, is the best part. (Wu-Tang Clan, "Wu-Revolution")

bibliography

Abbott, Edwin A. *A Shakespearian Grammar*. London: Macmillan, 1870.

Aitchison, Jean. *Words in the Mind: An Introduction to the Mental Lexicon*. Oxford: Blackwell, 1987.

Alford, Henry. *A Plea for the Queen's English*. London: Strahan, 1864.

Allen, John. *BBC News Styleguide*. London: BBC Training & Development, 2003. www2.media.uoa.gr/lectures/linguistic_archives/academic_ papers0506/notes/stylesheets_3.pdf.

Alvey, Edward Jr. "Individualizing in High-School English." *The English Journal*, 20, no. 2 (1931): 145–150.

American Heritage Dictionary of the English Language, 1st ed. Boston: Houghton Mifflin, 1969.

American Heritage Dictionary of the English Language, 5th ed. Boston: Houghton Mifflin, 2011.

Amis, Kingsley. *The King's English*. New York: Thomas Dunne Books, 1997.

Art and Science of Selling. Chicago: National Salesmens Training Association, 1922.

Ayres, Albert. *The Verbalist*. New York: Appleton, 1894.

Bache, Richard Meade. *Vulgarisms and Other Errors of Speech*. Philadelphia: Claxton, Remsen & Haffelfinger, 1868.

Baker, Robert. *Reflections on the English Language*. London: J. Bell, 1770.

Bennett, J. A. W. "Laurence Nowell's Vocabularium Saxonicum by Albert H. Marckwardt, Laurence Nowell." *Review of English Studies* n.s. 5, no. 20 (October 1954): 398–399.

Bernstein, Theodore. *The Careful Writer*. New York: Atheneum, 1965.

———. *Watch Your Language*. Manhasset, NY: Channel Press, 1958.

Bierce, Ambrose. *The Collected Works of Ambrose Bierce*. New York and Washington: Neale Publishing, 1912.

Blair, Hugh. *Essays on Rhetoric, Abridged Chiefly from Dr. Blair's Lectures on That Science*. Boston: Thomas & Andrews, 1797.

———. *Lectures on Rhetoric and Belles Lettres*. Vol. 1. Dublin: Whitestone, Colles, 1783.

Blank, Paula. "The Babel of Renaissance Engli_h." In *The Oxford History of English*. Edited by Lynda Mugglestone, pp. 212–239. Oxford: Oxford University Press, 2006.

Blount, Thomas. *Glossographia*. London: Thomas Newcomb, 1656.

Bodine, Ann. "Androcentrism in Prescriptive Grammar: Singular 'They, Sex-Indefinite He, and He or She.'" *Language in Society* 4, no. 2 (August 1975): 129–146.

Bolinger, Dwight. "It's so Fun." *American Speech* 38, no. 3 (October 1963): 236–240.

———. "Word Affinities." *American Speech* 15, no.1 (February 1940).

"Book Review." *The European Magazine and London Review* 12 (1787): 112–116.

Brackmann, Rebecca. *The Elizabethan Invention of Anglo-Saxon England: Studies in Renaissance Literature*. Cambridge, UK: D. S. Brewer, 2012.

Bremner, John. *Words on Words*. New York: Columbia University Press, 1980.

Brewer, Charlotte. "Shakespeare, Word-Coining, and the *OED*." *Shakespeare Survey* 65 (2013).

Brontë, Charlotte. *Jane Eyre: An Autobiography*. 2nd ed. London: Smith, Elder, 1848.

Bryant, Margaret. *Current American Usage*. New York: Funk & Wagnalls Company, 1962.

Bullions, Peter. *The Principles of English Grammar*. New York: Pratt, Woodford, 1834.

Bunce, Oliver Bell. *Don't: A Manual of Mistakes & Improprieties More or Less Prevalent in Conduct and Speech*. London: Field & Tuer, 1883.

Burchfield, Robert. *Points of View: Aspects of Present-Day English*. Oxford: Oxford University Press, 1992.

Burdon, William. *An Examination of the Merits and Tendency of the Pursuits of Literature, Part First*. Newcastle-upon-Tyne, UK: M. Brown, 1799.

Burgess, Thomas. *An Essay on the Study of Antiquities*. 2nd ed. Oxford: 1782.

Butler, Samuel. *Hudibras in Three Parts*. London: Rogers, 1684.

Calvin, Jean. *Sermons of Master Iohn Caluin, vpon the booke of Iob*. London: Harison & Byshop, 1574.

Campbell, George. *The Philosophy of Rhetoric*. Vol. 1. London: W. Strahan, 1776.

Catullus. *The Poems of Caius Valerius Catullus, in English Verse*. London: J. Johnson, 1795.

Central Record (Lancaster, KY), March 3, 1921, p. 6/2.

Chesterton, G. K. *The Appetite of Tyranny, Including Letters to an Old Garibaldian*. New York: Dodd, Mead, 1915.

Church of England. *Constitutio[ns] and Canons Ecclesiasticall Treated vpon by the Bishop of London*. London: Robert Baker, 1604.

Clements, Warren. "Coin to Blow and Coining Non-Words." *Globe and Mail* (Toronto), August 7, 2010, p. R8.

Cleveland Plain Dealer, May 9, 1890, p. 7.

Coles, Elisha. *An English Dictionary*. London: Peter Parker, 1677.

Collins, Gail. "More American Idols." *New York Times*, August 11, 2010. nytimes.com/2010/08/12/opinion/12collins.html?_r=0.

Comly, John. *English Grammar, Made Easy to the Teacher and Pupil*. Philadelphia: John H. Oswald for Emmor Kimber, 1803.

Constitutio[ns] and canons ecclesiasticall treated vpon by the Bishop of London. London: Robert Baker, 1604.

Copperud, Roy H. *American Usage and Style: The Consensus*. New York: Van Nostrand Reinhold, 1980.

Courtenay, Edward. *Courtenay's Dictionary of Abbreviations*. London: Groombridge and Sons, 1855.

Craig, Hugh. "Shakespeare's Vocabulary: Myth and Reality." *Shakespeare Quarterly* 62, no. 1 (Spring 2011): pp. 53–74.

The Critic: A Weekly Review of Literature and the Arts (New York), December 25, 1886, p. 318.

Crystal, David. *The Cambridge Encyclopedia of the English Language*. New York: Cambridge University Press, 1995.

———. *Think on My Words: Exploring Shakespeare's Language*. New York: Cambridge University Press, 2008.

———. *Txtng: The Gr8 Db8*. New York: Oxford University Press, 2008.

D'Arcy, Alexandra. "Like and Language Ideology: Disentangling Fact from Fiction." *American Speech* 82, no. 4 (Winter 2007): 386–419.

Dailey-O'Cain, Jennifer. "The Sociolinguistic Distribution Toward Focuser *Like* and Quotative *Like*." *Journal of Sociolinguistics* 4, no. 1 (2006): 60–80.

D'Anna, Catherine, Eugene Zechmeister, and James Hall. "Toward a Meaningful Definition of Vocabulary Size." *Journal of Reading Behavior*. Vol. XXIII (1991): 109–122.

Darwin, Charles. *The Descent of Man*. Princeton, NJ: Princeton University Press, 1981.

Dixon, R. M. W. "Comparative Constructions in English." *Studia Anglica Posnaniensia* 41 (2005): 5–27.

Documents of the School Committee of the City of Boston. Boston: City of Boston Printing Department, 1916.

"Dog Whines at Bad Grammar." *Washington Post*, January 7, 1908, p. 6.

Douglas, Gawin. *The XIII Bukes of Eneados of the Famose Poete Virgill*. London: William Copland, 1553.

Dryden, John. *The Conquest of Granada*. London: Henry Herringman, 1672.

———. *The Works of John Dryden, Revised and Corrected by George Saintsbury*. Vol. XVIII. London: William Paterson, 1893.

Elphinston, James. *The Principles of the English Language Digested*, Vol. II. London: James Bettenham, 1765.

Elyot, Thomas. *The education or bringeing vp of children*. London: Thomas Berthelet, 1532.

Encyclopaedia Britannica: Supplement to the Fourth, Fifth, and Sixth Editions. Edinburgh, UK: A. Constable, 1824.

Erasmus, Desiderius. *A Treatise Perswadynge a Man Patientlye to Suffre the Deth of His Frende*. London: Thomas Berthelet, 1531.

Fishback, Margaret. *I Take It Back: Verses*. New York: Dutton, 1935.

Follett, Wilson, and Erik Wensberg. *Modern American Usage*. New York: Hill & Wang, 1998.

Fowler, George and Henry Watson. *The King's English*. 2nd ed. Oxford: Clarendon Press, 1906.

Fowler, Henry. *A Dictionary of Modern English Usage*. Oxford: Clarendon Press, 1926.

Fox, George. *A Battle-Door for Teachers and Professors to Learn Singular & Plural*. London: Robert Wilson, 1660.

Garner, Bryan. *Garner's Modern American Usage*. New York: Oxford University Press, 2009.

Goldstein, Malcolm. "Pope, Sheffield, and Shakespeare's Julius Caesar." *Modern Language Notes* 71, no. 1 (1956): 8–10.

"Good Grammar or Good Taste?" *Wall Street Journal*, July 6, 1970, p. 8.

Greenwood, James. *A Royal English Grammar*. 2nd ed. London: J. Applebee, 1744.

———. *An Essay Towards a Practical English Grammar*. 5th ed. London: J. Nourse, 1753.

Harris, George. *Observations upon the English Language*. London: Edward Withers, 1752.

Hart, John Seely. *A Manual of Composition and Rhetoric: A Text-Book for Schools and Colleges*. Philadelphia: Eldredge & Brother, 1891.

Hartlib, Samuel. *A Further Discoverie of the Office of Publick Addresse for Accommodations*. London, 1648.

Heffer, Simon. *Strictly English: The Correct Way to Write . . . and Why It Matters*. London: Random House, 2011.

Hemingway, Ernest and A. E. Hotchner. *The Good Life According to Hemingway*. New York: HarperCollins, 2008.

Hesse, Monica. "AP's Approval of 'Hopefully' Symbolizes Larger Debate over Language." *Washington Post*, April 17, 2012. washingtonpost.com/lifestyle/style/aps-approval-of-hopefully-symbolizes-larger-debate-over-language/2012/04/17/gIQAti4zOT_story.html.

Hill, Thomas. *The Contemplation of Mankind*. London: William Seres, 1571.

Hirsch, D., and P. Nation. "What Vocabulary Size Is Needed to Read Unsimplified Texts for Pleasure?" In *Reading in a Foreign Language* 8 (1992): 689–696.

Hitchens, Christopher. *Thomas Paine's Rights of Man*. New York: Grove Press, 2006.

Hook, D. "The Apostrophe: Use and Misuse." *English Today* 15, no. 3 (July 1999): 42–49.

Hull, Joseph Hervey. *English Grammar by Lectures*. Boston: Lincoln and Edmands, 1828.

Hutchins, Joseph. *An Abstract of the First Principles of English Grammar*. Philadelphia: Thomas Dobson, 1791.

"Inaccuracies of Diction." *New England Magazine* 7 (1834): 469.

Jefferson, Thomas. *Notes on the State of Virginia*. Paris, 1782.

———. *The Writings of Thomas Jefferson*. Washington, DC: Taylor and Maury, 1853.

Johnson, Samuel. *A Dictionary of the English Language*. London: W. Strahan, 1755.

———. *The Plan of a Dictionary of the English Language*. London: J. and P. Knapton, et al., 1747.

———. *The Plays of William Shakespeare*. Vol. viii. London: J. and R. Tonson, 1764.

Johnson, Samuel, and Henry J. Todd. *A Dictionary of the English Language, with Additions by Henry J. Todd*. London: Longman, Hurst, Rees, Orme, & Brown, 1818.

Jonson, Ben. *The Workes of Beniamin Jonson*. London: W. Stansby, 1616.

"Kansas Notes." *Kansas City Star*, June 19, 1920, p. 10.

Knox, Jack. "A Political Platform Worth Fighting For." Prince George Citizen, February 15, 2005, p. 4.

Krapp, George. *Modern English: Its Growth and Present Use.* New York: Scribner's, 1909.

Lancaster, Emilie. *'Tween Heaven and Earth.* London: Remington, 1887.

Lane, Archibald. *A Key to the Art of Letter: or, English as a Learned Language.* London: Ralph Smith, 1705.

Langworth, Richard. *Churchill by Himself: the Definitive Book of Quotations.* New York: PublicAffairs, 2008.

Leonard, Sterling. *Current English Usage.* Chicago: Inland Press, 1932.

———. *Doctrine of Correctness in English Usage.* New York: Russell & Russell, 1962.

Longman Dictionary of Contemporary English. ldoceonline.com.

Lovechild, Mrs. *The Mother's Grammar.* London: John Marsaall, 1798.

Lowth, Robert. *A Short Introduction to English Grammar.* London: J. Hughs, 1762.

Macdonald, Dwight. "The String Untuned." *New Yorker,* March 10, 1962.

———. *A Moral Temper: The Letters of Dwight Macdonald.* Chicago: Ivan R. Dee, 2001.

Madan, A., S. Mehta, and Y. Dua. *Communication Skills in English.* New Delhi, India: V. K. Enterprises, 2011.

Mair, Christian. *Twentieth Century English: History, Variation and Standardization.* Cambridge: Cambridge University Press, 2006.

Manning, Ben. "Under Obama, We Can Expect 'Excessive Wickedness.'" *Indianapolis Star,* November 8, 2008.

Marryat, Frederick. *A Diary in America, with Remarks on Its Institutions.* Philadelphia: Carey & Hart, 1839.

Mason, C. P. *English Grammar: Including the Principles of Grammatical Analysis.* Toronto: Adam Miller, 1878.

Maxwell, William Henry. *Introductory Lessons in English Grammar.* New York and Chicago: A. S. Barnes, 1888.

McKnight, George and Bert Emsley. *Modern English in the Making.* New York: D. Appleton, 1928.

Mearns, Hughes. *The Vinegar Saint.* Philadelphia: Penn Publishing, 1919.

Meiklejohn, John. *The Art of Writing English.* London: A. M. Holden, 1899.

Mencken, H. L. *The American Language.* New York: Knopf, 1919.

"Merck's Correspondence." *Dublin University Magazine,* October 1838, p. 401.

Merriam-Webster's New International Dictionary. Springfield, MA: Merriam-Webster, 1909.

Merriam-Webster's Third New International Dictionary. Springfield, MA: Merriam-Webster, 1961.

Merriam-Webster's Collegiate Dictionary. 11th ed. Springfield, MA: Merriam-Webster, 2004.

Merriam-Webster Dictionary of English Usage. Springfield, MA: Merriam-Webster, 1989.

Miège, Guy. *A Short Dictionary, English and French.* London: 1684.

Monroe, B. S. "An English Academy." *Modern Philology* 8, no. 1 (July 1910): 107–122.

Montagu, Walter. *The Shepheard's Paradise.* London: Thomas Dring, 1629.

Moon, George Washington. *The Bad English of Lindley Murray and Other Writers.* London: Hatchard, 1868.

Morris, William, and Mary Morris. *Harper's Dictionary of Contemporary Usage.* New York: Harper & Row, 1975.

Morton, Herbert. *The Story of Webster's Third.* New York: Cambridge University Press, 1994.

"Murdering English," *Evening Missourian* (Columbia), March 5, 1921, p. 4/1.

Murray, Lindley. *English Grammar, Adapted to the Different Classes of Learners.* London: York, 1799.

Nabokov, Vladimir. *Invitation to a Beheading.* New York: Putnam's, 1959.

Nagy, W. and R. Anderson. "How Many Words Are There in Printed English?" *Reading Research Quarterly* Vol. 19 (1984): 304–330.

Nesfield, John. *English Grammar: Past and Present.* London: Macmillan, 1898.

New Oxford American Dictionary. 3rd ed. New York: Oxford University Press, 2010.

Newton, Isaac. *The Mathematical Principles of Natural Philosophy.* Vol. 2. London: Benjamin Motte, 1729.

"Objectionable Usage," *Medicine Hat News* (Alberta, Canada), March 9, 1921, p. 2/3.

O'Connor, Johnson. "Vocabulary and Success." *Atlantic Monthly,* January 1934, pp. 160–166.

"On Lord Beauchamp's Bill." *Public Advertiser,* April 24, 1780, pp. 2–3.

Orwell, George. "*Tribune,* December 24, 1943." In *All Art Is Propaganda: Critical Essays.* New York; Houghton Mifflin Harcourt, 2008.

Oxford Companion to the English Language. New York: Oxford University Press, 1992.

Oxford Dictionary of National Biography. Edited by Leslie Stephen. London: Smith, Elder & Co., 1885.

Oxford English Dictionary. oed.com.

Palgrave, Francis Turner. *Landscape in Poetry from Homer to Tennyson*. London: Macmillan, 1897.

Papers and Proceedings of the Thirty Second Annual Meeting of the American Library Association. Chicago: American Library Association, 1910.

Parkes, M. B. *Pause and Effect: An Introduction to the History of Punctuation in the West*. Berkeley: University of California Press, 1993.

Perrin, Porter G. and Wilma R. Ebbitt. *Writer's Guide and Index to English*. 5th ed. Glenview, IL: Scott, Foresman, 1972.

Poems on the Four Last Things. London: Thomas Ballard, 1706.

Popper, Karl. *The Open Society and Its Enemies*. 5th ed. Princeton, NJ: Princeton University Press, 1971.

Pound, Ezra. *The Selected Letters of Ezra Pound, 1907–1941*. New York: Harcourt Brace Jovanovich, 1950.

Procter, Ben. *William Randolph Hearst: The Early Years, 1863–1910*. New York: Oxford University Press, 1998.

Quackenbos, G. P. *Advanced Course of Composition and Rhetoric*. New York: D. Appleton, 1857.

The Queen's English Society. queens-english-society.com.

The Queen's English Society. "What We Can Do." queens-english-society.com/about_contd.html.

Read, A. W. "American Projects for an Academy to Regulate Speech." *PMLA* 51 (December 1936): 1141–1179.

Ritter, R. M. *New Hart's Rule: The Handbook of Style for Writers and Editors*. Oxford: Oxford University Press, 2005.

Robie, Walter Franklin. *Sex and Life*. Boston: Gorham Press, 1920.

Roosevelt, Franklin Delano. *F.D.R.: His Personal Letters*. New York: Duell, Sloan, & Pearce, 1970.

Roosevelt, Theodore. *The Rough Riders*. New York: Putnam's, 1900.

Royal, Brandon. *The Little Gold Grammar Book: Mastering the Rules That Unlock the Power of Writing*. Calgary: Maven, 2010.

Scase, Wendy. "Pecock, Reginald (*b. c.* 1392, *d.* in or after 1459)." In *Oxford Dictionary of National Biography*. New York: Oxford University Press, 2004. oxforddnb.com/view/article/21749.

Schmich, Mary. "Obama Speech Sparks Misuse of Enormous Proportions." *Chicago Tribune*, January 23, 2009. articles.chicagotribune.com/2009-01-23/news/0901230121_1_housing-crisis-pest-enormity.

Scott, Walter. "Scott's Edition of Swift." *Edinburgh Review*, September 1816.

Seashore, R. H., and L. D. Eckerson. "The Measurement of Individual Differences in General English Vocabularies." *Journal of Educational Psychology* 31, no. 1 (January 1940).

Skelton, John. *A Replycacion Agaynst Certayne Yong Scolers Abjured of Late.* London: Richard Pynson, ca. 1528.

Skinner, David. *The Story of Ain't.* New York: Harper, 2012.

Sklar, Elizabeth S. "The Possessive Apostrophe: The Development and Decline of a Crooked Mark." *College English* 38, no. 2 (1976): 175–83.

Sledd, James, and Wilma Ebbitt. *Dictionaries and That Dictionary.* Chicago: Scott, Foresman, 1962.

"Smashing English," *Public Ledger* (Maysville, KY), February 28, 1921, p. 2/1.

Smith, C. Alphono. "The Order of Words in Anglo-Saxon Prose." *PMLA* 8, no. 2 (1893).

The Speaker: A Review of Politics, Letters, Science, and the Arts. London, July 4, 1891, p. 12.

Stout, Rex. *Black Orchids.* New York: Grosset & Dunlop, 1942.

Strunk, William Jr. *The Elements of Style.* New York: Harcourt, Brace and Company, 1918.

Strunk, William Jr., and E. B. White. *The Elements of Style.* New York: Macmillan, 1959.

Swift, Jonathan. *A Proposal for Correcting, Improving and Ascertaining the English Tongue.* London: Benjamin Tooke, 1712.

"The Three-Timers." *The Gazette* (Fort Worth, TX), June 14, 1891, p. 16/6.

Tressler, Jacob Cloyd. *English in Action.* Boston & New York: Heath, 1929.

Tuke, Thomas. *Concerning the Holy Eucharist.* Amsterdam: Successors of G. Thorp, 1625.

Turner, Brandon. *A New English Grammar.* London: Scott, Webster, & Geary, 1840.

"Typographical Art." *Puck,* March 30, 1881.

University of Arizona Writing Center. "Prepositions." studentsuccess.asu .edu/sites/default/files/Prepositions.pdf.

University of Iowa. "Common Errors to Avoid on Term Papers." uiowa .edu/~c014014/tips.html.

University of Nevada Writing Center. "Writing Tips: Prepositions." writing center.unlv.edu/writing/prepositions.html.

Utley, Garrick. *You Should Have Been Here Yesterday: A Life Story in Television News.* New York: Diane Publishing, 2000.

Vindex Anglicus; or, The Perfections of the English Language Defended, and Asserted. Oxford: Henry Hall, 1644.

Visser, Fredericus Theodorus. *An Historical Syntax of the English Language.* Parts 1–3. The Netherlands: Brill, 1963.

Wallace, David Foster. *Both Flesh and Not: Essays.* New York: Little, Brown and Co., 2012.

Walpole, Horace. *Letters of Horace Walpole, Earl of Oxford, to Sir Horace Mann, His Britannic Majesty's Resident at the Court of Florence, from 1760 to 1785.* Vol. 2. London: Richard Bentley, 1843.

Webster, Noah. *Dissertations on the English Language: With Notes, Historical and Critical.* Boston: Isaiah Thomas, 1789.

———. *A Grammatical Institute of the English Language.* Hartford: Hudson & Goodwin, 1784.

Wells, William Harvey. *Wells's School Grammar.* New York: Ivison & Phinney, 1859.

Wendell, Barrett. *English Composition, Eight Lectures Given at the Lowell Institute.* New York: Scribner's, 1891.

Wharton, Jeremiah. *The English-Grammar.* London: William Dugard, 1654.

White, E. B. "Talk of the Town." *New Yorker,* March 27, 1965.

White, Richard Grant. *Words and Their Uses, Past and Present.* 5th ed. Boston: Houghton Mifflin, 1882.

Will, George. *Roundtable.* ABC News transcript, May 27, 2012.

Wills, Garry. "Madness in Their Method." *National Review,* February 13, 1962.

———. *Nixon Agonistes: The Crisis of the Self-Made Man.* Boston: Houghton Mifflin, 1969.

Wogalter, M. S., et al. "Hazard Connotation of Fire Safety Terms." *Proceedings of the Human Factors and Ergonomics Society 54th Annual Meeting, 2010*: 1837–1840.

Wright, Joseph. *A Philosophical Grammar of the English Language.* New York: Spinning & Hodges, 1838.

Yáñez-Bouza, Nuria. "Preposition Stranding and Prescriptivism in English from 1500 to 1900: A Corpus-Based Approach." (PhD Thesis, University of Manchester), 2007.

Zimmer, Ben. "A Misattribution No Longer to Be Put Up With." Language Log, December 12, 2004. itre.cis.upenn.edu/~myl/languagelog/archives/001715.html.

notes

INTRODUCTION

1 Bodine, pp. 131–33.

CHAPTER 1: ARGUING SEMANTICS

1 Tweet, 8:22 a.m., April 17, 2012. twitter.com/APStylebook/status/192241618592595969.
2 Hesse, Web.
3 Morris and Morris, p. 311.
4 E. B. White, p. 35.
5 *Cleveland Plain Dealer*, p. 7.
6 *Dublin University Magazine*, p. 401.
7 Hartlib, p. 1.
8 Copperud, p. 185.
9 Follett and Wensberg, p. 144.
10 Bremner, p. 192.
11 Nabokov, p. 19.
12 T. Roosevelt, p. 18.
13 Montagu, p. 136.
14 Miège, "disinteressé."
15 Blount, "decimate."
16 Coles, "decimate."

17 Ayres, p. 42.
18 Schmich, Web.
19 Manning, Ben. Letter to editor, Web.
20 Heffer, p. 144.
21 Elyot, unpaginated.
22 O'Connor, p. 160.
23 Erasmus, p. 15.
24 Johnson and Todd, "Unique."
25 Burgess, p. 43.
26 Scott, p. 9.
27 *Encyclopaedia Britannica*, p. 68.
28 Fowler (1906), p. 58.
29 Royal, p. 169.
30 *New Oxford American Dictionary*, "unique."
31 *Merriam-Webster's Collegiate Dictionary*, "unique."
32 *Longman Dictionary of Contemporary English*, "unique."
33 *American Heritage Dictionary of the English Language*, 5th ed., "unique."
34 Brontë, p. x.
35 Pound, p. 50.
36 Walpole, p. 199.
37 Palgrave, p. 220.
38 Douglas, unpaginated.
39 Orwell, p. 202.
40 Hitchens, p. 133.
41 Goldstein, p. 9.
42 Popper, p 36.
43 Newton, p. 207.
44 Darwin, p. 150.
45 Murray, p. 137.
46 Wright, pp. 51–52.
47 Amis, p. 235.

CHAPTER 2: WORDS THAT ARE NOT WORDS

1 Jefferson, p. 118.
2 "Book Review."
3 Fowler (1926), p. 47.
4 Bernstein (1965), p. 65.
5 Bernstein (1958), p. 76.
6 Morris, 1975, p. 48.

7 Dixon, pp. 5–27.
8 Nesfield, p. 336.
9 Tuke, p. 7.
10 Catullus, p. 63.
11 Pound, p. 158.
12 Chesterton, p. 101.
13 Maxwell, p. 64.
14 Bolinger (1940), pp. 69–70.
15 "The Three-Timers," p. 16/6.
16 Clements, p. R8
17 Lancaster, p. 26.

CHAPTER 3: VERBING NOUNS

1 Allen, Web.
2 Knox, p. 1.
3 Will, unpaginated.
4 "On Lord Beauchamp's Bill," pp. 2–3.
5 Smith, p. 237.
6 Mencken, p. 194.
7 Stout, p. 63.
8 Church of England, unpaginated.
9 *Poems on the Four Last Things*, p. 70.
10 "Jibes of 'Contact' as a Verb," p. 32.
11 Strunk and White, p. 68.

CHAPTER 4: SINS OF GRAMMAR

1 Bache, p. 68.
2 "Dog Whines at Bad Grammar," p. 6.
3 Visser, pp. 1036–37.
4 "Inaccuracies of Diction," p. 469.
5 Comly, p. 122.
6 Visser, pp. 1040–44.
7 W. Scase, Web.
8 Butler, p. 248.
9 Visser, p. 1024.
10 *Papers and Proceedings*, p. 613.
11 Fowler and Watson, p. 319.
12 Meiklejohn, p. 251.

13 Baker, p. iv.
14 Ibid., p. ii.
15 Mair, p. 19.
16 Johnson (1764), p. 423.
17 Hemingway and Hotchner, p. 111.
18 Greenwood (1753), p. 6.
19 Burdon, p. 12.
20 Quackenbos, p. 88.
21 Moon, p. 95.
22 Ibid.
23 Greenwood (1744), p. 161.
24 Strunk (1918), p. 40.
25 Documents of the School Committee of the City of Boston, p. 17.
26 *Art and Science of Selling*, p. 52.
27 Taylor, p. 457.
28 Burchfield, p. 109.
29 Johnson (1755).
30 Bolinger (1963), p. 236.
31 Harris, pp. 19–20.
32 *Merriam-Webster Dictionary of English Usage*, p. 894.
33 Alford, p. 90.
34 Wells, p. 63.
35 Fowler (1906), p. 81.
36 Fowler (1926), 635.
37 Ritter, p. 67.
38 Wallace, p. 265.
39 Perrin & Ebbitt, p. 725.
40 Dryden (1672), p. 165.
41 Dryden (1893), p. 181.
42 Lowth, p. 127–28.
43 Lane, p. 93.
44 Blair (1783), p. 285.
45 Webster (1784), p. 79.
46 Turner, p. 229.
47 Yáñez-Bouza, p. 256.
48 Lovechild, p. 56.
49 Blair (1797), p. 92.
50 Hart, p. 136.
51 *American Heritage Dictionary* (2011), "preposition."
52 Garner, p. 654.

53 Strunk and White, p. 70.

54 University of Nevada, Web.

55 University of Arizona, Web.

56 University of Iowa, Web.

57 Madan et al., p. 22.

58 Wendell, p. 80.

59 *Central Record*, p. 6.

60 "Murdering English," p. 4/1.

61 Smashing English," p. 2/1.

62 "Objectionable Usage," p. 2/3.

63 Fowler, p. 346.

64 *Merriam-Webster New International Dictionary* (1909).

65 Leonard (1932), p. 108.

66 Crystal (1995), p. 194.

67 Fox, unpaginated.

68 Leonard (1962), p. 187.

69 *OED*, "good," sense 3c.

CHAPTER 5:
THE CONTINUING DETERIORATION OF THE LANGUAGE

1 Swift, p. 8.

2 Amis (1997), p. 14.

3 Hook, p. 44.

4 Parkes, p. 138, n. 75.

5 Oxford Companion to the English Language, p. 75.

6 Harris, p. 22.

7 Mason, p. 29.

8 Krapp, pp. 86–87.

9 Wharton, p. 54.

10 "It may not be amiss to engage potatoe seed," in a letter to James Cleveland, January 10, 1775.

11 "[T]he entire mass of organizable matter might be converted into a single species of plants, the potatoe for example," in a letter to George Featherstonhaugh, December 23, 1820.

12 "I gave them a hot potatoe," in *Correspondence of Andrew Jackson*, p. 6–7: 142.

13 "A gentleman of my own staff has paid a dollar for a dinner which consisted of a single potatoe and a piece of beef and bread that being all he could get," in *The Papers of Ulysses S. Grant*, p. 12:464.

14 "[F]or I find occassionally a potatoe eaten by the lime," in *The Diary of James A. Garfield,* p. 313.

15 F. D. Roosevelt, p. 75.

16 Procter, p. 4.

17 Alvey, pp. 148–49.

18 Bierce, p. 387.

19 *Webster's Third New International Dictionary,* p. 45.

20 Macdonald (1962), p. 148.

21 Wills (1962), p. 98.

22 Macdonald (2001), p. 443.

23 Wills (1969), p. 217.

24 Marryat, p. 154.

25 Ibid.

26 R. White, p. 181.

27 Ibid.

28 Bache, pp. 34–35.

29 Robie, p. 220

30 Mearns, p. 24.

31 White (1882), p. 94.

32 Bunce, p. 74.

33 Bunce, p. 78.

34 Utley, p. 4.

35 Fishback, p. 117.

36 Elphinston, p. 463.

37 Hutchins, p. 158.

38 Bullions, 1834.

39 *The Speaker,* p. 12.

40 *The Critic,* p. 318.

41 "Good Grammar or Good Taste?," p. 8.

42 D'Arcy, pp. 386–419.

43 Dailey-O'Cain, p. 73.

CHAPTER 6: DEFENDING ENGLISH

1 Brackmann, p. 72.

2 Bennett, pp. 398–99.

3 Brackmann, pp 57–58.

4 Blank, p. 275.

5 *Vindex anglicus,* unpaginated.

6 Webster (1789), p. 222.

7 Campbell, 412.

8 Langworth, p. 61.

9 Fowler and Watson, p. 7.

10 Skelton, unpaginated.

11 Harris, pp. 13–14.

12 Monroe, pp. 1–2.

13 Johnson (1747), p. 32.

14 Johnson (1755), p. 5.

15 Cited in Monroe, p. 15.

16 Read, p. 1144.

17 Ibid., pp. 1145–46.

18 Ibid., p. 1151.

19 Queen's English Society, Web.

20 Ibid.

21 Hirsch and Nation, pp. 689–96.

22 Dana et al., pp. 109–22.

23 Nagy and Anderson, pp. 304–30.

24 Seashore and Eckerson, pp. 14-38.

25 Aitchison, p. 7.

26 Calvin, unpaginated.

27 Hill, unpaginated.

28 Brewer, pp. 345–57.

29 Craig, p. 8.

30 Crystal (2008), p. 2.

31 Abbott, pp. 295–320.

32 McKnight and Emsley, p. 169.

index

about the author

Photo by Ogden Thelonious Horowitz Shea

Ammon Shea is the author of several books on English vocabulary, including *Reading the OED* and *Depraved and Insulting English,* as well as *The Phone Book.* He has worked as consulting editor on American dictionaries for Oxford University Press, and as a reader for the North American Reading Program of the Oxford English Dictionary. He lives in New York City with his wife (a former lexicographer), son (a potential future lexicographer), and two nonlexical dogs.